BUSINESS MODEL RENEWAL

BUSINESS MODEL RENEWAL

HOW TO GROW AND PROSPER BY DEFYING BEST PRACTICES AND REINVENTING YOUR STRATEGY

LINDA GORCHELS

McGraw Hill

New York Chicago San Francisco Lisbon London Madrid Mexico City
New Delhi San Juan Seoul Singapore Sydney Toronto

The McGraw-Hill Companies

1 2 3 4 5 6 7 8 9 0 QFR/QFR 1 8 7 6 5 4 3 2

ISBN: 978-0-07-178403-0
MHID: 0-07-178403-9

e-ISBN: 978-0-07-178404-7
e-MHID: 0-07-178404-7

This book is printed on acid-free paper.

CONTENTS

Author's Note

It seems appropriate for a book on business model renewal to be part of a larger business model shift in publishing. This one is. It is available in two formats: the traditional paper version, and in e-book format—the very format that is changing publishing—which will in some cases allow you to link directly from the book to video clips on the Web.

I configured the book in much the same way that I create executive education classes as part of the University of Wisconsin–Madison's School of Business. When I work with mid-career managers, executives, and professionals, I am fully aware of the challenge for them to stay focused (quiescently) for a three-day course. (After all, you are hyper-connected, busy people used to being on the move at all times.) Consequently, for me to be fully effective, I augment my discourse with video clips, guest lectures, and various thinking activities. In other words, I expand beyond my own perspectives to provide a richer experience for my clients. While this work is the sum of my interactions with thousands of people around the world as a consultant and facilitator, I am constantly adding new insights from others. I incorporated many of these same techniques into this book. The end-of-chapter interviews are the metaphorical "guest lectures," and many of the Web connections are identical to the ones I use at the university.

You'll notice numerous hyperlinks to video clips in nearly all chapters. The hyperlinks are live in the e-book version of the book on those devices that support access to the Web. In the print version and e-book version on devices that do not support access to the Web, the URLs that are "hidden" behind the selected hyperlink phrases are presented in a box near the relevant passage in the text. I will periodically monitor the links and post revisions as necessary on my website, Brain Snacks Café (www.brainsnackscafe.com/), or on my Amazon author's page. Please let me know if you have any additional Web resources that might be helpful for other readers, or if you have difficulty with any of the links. (As of February 2012, all links were functional.)

So challenge yourself to question your own perspectives (and mine!), and then establish an authentic framework for business model structure, growth, and renewal built on a broader set of ideas than you may have used in the past. Good luck!

Prologue

Do the following events indicate the end of "business as usual"?

- A recent statement on the home page of the Sony cassette Walkman indicated that its production is finished–more than 30 years after its debut in 1979.
- Wal-Mart has ended its strategy of using DVDs as traffic drivers–due to the impact of video-on-demand and Redbox kiosks.
- Advertising revenue is slowly moving from "traditional" media to digital media, having a significant impact on the survival of numerous magazines and broadcasting companies.
- At one time General Motors attempted to have separate brands "for every purse and purpose." But after reducing its portfolio–shedding Oldsmobile, Pontiac, Saturn, and others–it is left with four brands (Chevrolet, Cadillac, Buick, and GMC) and a reduction in the number of models.
- According to BankruptcyData.com, of the 20 largest public company bankruptcy filings in the last 30 years, 17 have occurred since 2001.

Yes, the end of business as we know it has been forecast many times. Many industries and approaches have indeed become obsolete. But companies continue to succeed and fail, innovate and degenerate, grow and decline. Is there a "secret" to success? Is it the business model … or the strategy … or the leadership … or the knowledge … or just being at the right place at the right time?

Obviously, all of these factors play a role–or stated more accurately, the factors play different roles under different circumstances. But before I get into the contextual differences I want to take a step back to look at terminology. It's interesting to listen to people defining the various terms related to business strategies and models. Even within the same company what one individual calls a business model another calls a strategy; what one calls a strategy another calls a tactic; what one calls a vision statement another calls a mission statement; what one calls leadership another calls management. There are no perfect or foolproof definitions. In theory and in practice the terms are used inconsistently. The only time the different definitions are troublesome is when they cause a breakdown in communication due to fundamental misinterpretations.

Nevertheless, as a starting point, I'd like to define these terms, while being fully aware there will always be variations in meanings as circumstances and cultures change. There is no solid line separating a business model and a strategy—it is more of a continuum—and in the book I will often be referencing the gray area in the middle. Similarly, goals can blur into objectives and strategies into tactics. So keep in mind, this is just a starting point.

Business model:	The totality of how a firm produces value—including strategy, organizational design, infrastructure, culture, and operational processes. It implicitly takes into account the ability to profitably execute strategy, and is consequently broader and more comprehensive than a strategy. When Eastman Kodak, over the past couple of decades, shifted the emphasis of its business model to digital cameras and accessories, it was really a change in DNA for the company. It competed not just with a different product strategy, but through a different way of doing business (even though still delivering on the "Kodak Moment").
Vision:	A fuzzy representation of a future state—what the firm aspires to become. It is a theme, a direction that should be infused throughout the business models, strategies, and plans. It is an indistinct (yet comprehensible) goal that might or might not be actually accomplished. Some companies refer to a vision statement as analogous to the beginning of the president's letter to shareholders in a future annual report.
Mission:	A firm's reason for existence; its core purpose. It often states the essential values and philosophies of a company.
Goal:	The desired end-result of a plan (the long-term *what),* generally a broad indication of a firm's direction. It is more specific than a vision and is more of a "promise" intended to be attained. (Visions are generally higher-level aspirations.)
Strategy:	A long-term plan of action to achieve a goal (the long-term *how*). From a military perspective a strategy is often considered the plan to win the war whereas tactics are considered the actions taken to win a battle.
Objective:	The desired end-result of a short-term plan (the short-term *what)* to move toward the long-term vision and goals.

An objective is generally more specific and concretely measurable than a goal, and should link annual plans to long-term strategic plans. It answers the question*: what am I going to accomplish this year to move closer to the long-term goal from where I am right now?*

Tactic: A short-term action or activity to achieve an objective (the short-term *how*). Some tactics are proactive and some are reactive, addressing current environmental realities that might not have been clear at the time a strategy was developed.

Leadership: Guidance through directional changes. According to John Kotter: *"Leadership and management are two distinctive and complementary systems of action.*

Management is about coping with complexity. Leadership is about coping with change." Based on this depiction, solid leadership is critical in leading a change to a new business model (or strategy) and management is required to implement the complexity of the change.

Management: Administration of complexity. It involves planning, budgeting, and controlling. While there is overlap between leadership and management, the first deals more with alignment and the latter with execution. Management is more about the day-to-day activities of getting work done.

Strategic foresight: The ability to monitor key, relevant trends in a way that enables awareness of multiple plausible futures. This may include scenario planning, systems thinking, and other tools.

Culture: The collective "personality" of an organization based on its core values, work philosophies, and expectations of managers and employees. The ability to shift strategies and/or create new business models will be made easier or more difficult based on the fit with the culture.

Change management: An approach to leading and managing the efforts to transition a firm through disruption—from its current state to a desired future state.

Disrupted: Thrown into turmoil. Business models (and strategies) can be thrown into disruption by a host of external factors including new technology, shifts in customer behavior, macroeconomic downturns, or even new competition. Organizations (and their leadership) must decide how to continue to grow or progress in the face of these potential disruptions.

The September 26, 2007 *Wall Street Journal* carried an article about the book, *From Higher Aims to Hired Hands*, by Harvard Business School professor, Rakesh Khurana. Prof. Khurana argued that business schools "have lost track of their original mission to produce far-sighted leaders … and the logic of stewardship has disappeared." The book posits that "panoramic, long-term thinking has given way to an almost grotesque obsession with maximizing shareholder value over increasingly brief spans." That fact, along with dramatic economic and technological changes, makes it critical for companies to reassess their business models and growth strategies.

Growth (or progress) does not resemble a staircase as much as a switchback road. Opportunities and threats will be hidden in plain sight, and some will be seemingly contradictory. Yet, firms must be open to ongoing transitions in the marketplace and to changes in customer behavior. For example, how many people now *listen* to books and *read* cell phones? A handful of relatively simple events like these can change your business (and even your life).

A decision has great merit when it is based on knowledge of both potential *future* consequences and collaborative *current* events. Executives are faced with numerous business decisions that require sacrificing either long-term results or short-term gain. A single decision, in other words, can become a catalyst for a variety of outcomes. Just as adding a domino to the "right" set-up of blocks and giving a gentle push can cause them all to tumble—a chain reaction often referred to as *the domino effect*—a current decision can have a long tail of results.

The reverse is also true. Carrying the domino analogy one step further, a set of dominoes will not fall down if one or several pieces are missing—an obstructed chain reaction I refer to as *the domino defect*. In other words, a current strategy or business model can fail if a necessary requirement is not in place. The implication: decision makers must learn how to think broadly to assess when the timing is right to execute a particular strategy and/or move to a different business model.

It will become clear that recreating the wheel is usually not necessary in business rethinking. There are a tremendous number of tools that can be used, but not all tools are appropriate for all jobs. So, let's roll up our sleeves and take a look at the myths and realities of strategies and business models … and what it means for your business.

BUSINESS MODEL RENEWAL

PART 1

Establishing Context

This part of the book introduces the framework for business model renewal. The first chapter describes the context, the decisions, and the alignment necessary for effective business model evaluation and planning. The second chapter summarizes and integrates various contemporary (as well as traditional) approaches to strategic planning and insights, and then builds them into a business model growth portfolio model.

CHAPTER 1

Defy Best Practices

When I was contracted to go to Eastern Europe to teach managers after the fall of the Berlin Wall, I took with me my toolbox of best practices. I addressed the principles of business acumen, segmentation, and planning. The classes in Poland and Hungary consisted of individuals from various management levels in a broad cross section of industries, yet the approach to strategy fit and benchmarking against world-class competitors was appropriate. I was impressed by the entrepreneurial drivc of the audience members; it came not from a high-tech innovative perspective but from a desire to start their own businesses.

Several years later I taught a series of classes in Shanghai and Beijing. The managers in the audience were from multinational corporations, and many had received their degrees in Australia and Europe. They were interested in developing more skills based on Western business practices to apply in very large organizations.

Although these situations were different in many ways, the common element was the thirst for best practices, and the capacity to learn and grow from them was incontrovertible. Yet a lot has happened over the last two decades—significant technological metamorphosis, transnational fluctuations, demographic shifts, and other upheavals—that has prompted a rethinking of business as usual. This doesn't mean that everything from the past must be thrown out, but it does imply a more nuanced approach to the basics.

Best practice is an elusive term. Some people use it to define actions (often taken by exemplar firms) that are presumed to be the reasons for a firm's success. Others use it to justify following a prescribed set of protocols that they believe improve performance. In some cases these best practices are indeed linked to superior performance, and in other cases they are based on historical interpretations or assumptions of cause and effect.

Although there are arguably examples of best-practice *tactics* or best-practice *processes*, can the term be applied to *strategies* and *business models*? That becomes more challenging since there so many interrelated pieces to the puzzle. Businesses operate within ecosystems that influence (although they do not necessarily predetermine) success or failure. The outcomes of a firm's strategy or a business model are not independent of its environment. Yet many executives and managers examine key success factors (perceived best practices) in excruciating detail without really exploring the interrelationships among the factors or between the factors and the environment. Peter Drucker once pointed out that "eventually every theory of the business becomes obsolete and then invalid" (cited at the Drucker Institute website). Thus, chances for success are increased when executives become contextual leaders, making and implementing decisions on the basis of the context of the situation.

Traditional approaches to strategy assumed a fairly stable and predictable world. This is no longer the case, and market leadership no longer guarantees profitability. Companies increasingly need an adaptive corporate culture, along with acceptance and appreciation of experimentation, to have a competitive advantage. Since experimentation necessarily produces failures (along with wins), there must be a tolerance of failure.

CONNECT STRATEGIES AND BUSINESS MODELS

Let's revisit my definitions of *strategy* and *business model* from the prologue. A strategy is a long-term plan of action to achieve a goal. A business model refers to the totality of the way a firm produces value, including strategy, organizational design, infrastructure, culture, and operational processes. It implicitly takes into account the ability to execute strategy profitably and is consequently broader and more comprehensive than a strategy.

However, sometimes the relationship between a strategy and a business model is confusing or inconsistent. Here are a couple of examples. Many years ago I worked for a company that was being considered for acquisition by other firms in its industry. I was invited to be part of a leveraged buyout. The strategy for the firm appropriately established a potential competitive advantage in the industry, but the business model (including organizational structure and resources) was not consistent with the strategy. There was a disconnect between the strategy and the business model required to operationalize the strategy. I declined the offer, and the firm folded shortly afterward.

Let's look at the book publishing industry as another example. Firms in traditional trade book publishing are manufacturers that make products from a variety of materials, including paper. Another major raw material consists of words coming from suppliers (authors). The publishers convert the raw material into printed or digitized books and sell the books through their channels, such as online aggregators such as Amazon and traditional resellers such as Barnes & Noble. The editing, design, manufacturing, and distribution are the "value-add" of the publisher, for which the author is paid a royalty. That is the traditional business model. As long as new product strategy changes are incremental, they can survive with this model. But what if new product strategy is more drastic? Will the existing business model still work?

For example, if the strategy is to create enhanced multiplatform books, perhaps modifications in the business model are warranted. Let's say the authors now provide not just words but also embedded video and presentations; the editing and design functions of the publisher now change from standard copyediting to audiovisual and technology support. New competencies must be built into the business model. Also, the fact that the raw material being purchased incorporates intellectual property that goes beyond words may cause a rethinking of the contractual relationship between the author and the publisher. If the book morphs from a printed product to a multiplatform product, the value-add of the publisher may shift either to broader electronic editing and design functions or to the role of web-based intermediary. In any event, a change in strategy may or may not require a reexamination of business models to ensure alignment between those functions.

Sometimes fluctuations in the external environment will require a change in strategy or a change in strategy will require a rethinking of the business model. That is why it's important to use best practices and success stories as sources of inspiration rather than as prescriptive how-to manuals.

CONSIDER THE ECOSYSTEM OF SUCCESS

What are *world-class* companies? Do they have larger revenues as evidenced by their presence on the Fortune 500 or a comparable list? Do they have better stock performance? Is their brand image stronger? Are they growing more quickly? Have they received recognition by their peers (or third parties) for being world class? Do they have stronger relationships with customers and employees? Do they use a balanced scorecard or espouse sustainability? What is the role of corporate culture and current external factors? Can any company become world class simply by following a prescribed set of best practices? Or does it require being an innovative disruptor?

These are not easily answered questions. However, I have worked with many professionals who doggedly seek out world-class best practices and occasionally force-fit them into their organizations. They may believe there is a single right approach and often minimize the due diligence necessary to learn the preferred approach for them at a particular point in time.

Let's explore some potential criteria that *might* be used to identify world-class companies, beginning with presence on the Fortune 500. *Fortune* magazine lists the largest corporations in terms of revenue. To be included, a company must be incorporated in the United States and file financial statements with a government agency. Between 1955 (when *Fortune* first began the 500 list) and 2011, there have been over 2,100 companies on the list. Only around 3 percent of them have been on the list from the beginning. Others were on the list for a few or several years before going private, being acquired by another company, or going out of business. Still others have more recently attained the size to become part of the list.

If we look only at the top 25 on the list (Table 1-1), we see subtle changes over the years. In 1955 the top companies were heavily dominated by auto-

Table 1-1

Comparative Fortune 500 Rankings

	Top 25 in 1955	Top 25 in 2011
1	General Motors	Walmart Stores
2	Exxon Mobil	Exxon Mobil
3	U.S. Steel	Chevron
4	General Electric	ConocoPhillips
5	Esmark	Fannie Mae
6	Chrysler	General Electric
7	Armour	Berkshire Hathaway
8	Gulf Oil	General Motors
9	Mobil	Bank of America
10	DuPont	Ford Motor
11	Amoco	Hewlett-Packard
12	Bethlehem Steel	AT&T
13	CBS	J.P. Morgan Chase & Co.
14	Texaco	Citigroup
15	AT&T Technologies	McKesson
16	Shell Oil	Verizon Communications
17	Kraft	American International Group
18	Chevron Texaco	IBM
19	Goodyear Tire & Rubber	Cardinal Health
20	Boeing	Freddie Mac
21	Sinclair Oil	CVS Caremark
22	Navistar International	UnitedHealth Group
23	RCA	Wells Fargo
24	Union Carbide	Valero Energy
25	Firestone Tire and Rubber	Kroger

motive, oil, steel, and other industrial firms. Although some of those companies were still present in 2011, it's not surprising that technology, financial services, and retail/wholesale have grown in significance. Although I've listed only the top 25, similar observations can be made about the rest of the Fortune 500 and corporate America in general. Best practices arguably have changed as these shifts have occurred, and that doesn't take into account what might be the requirements for emerging technology and bioscience companies.

Obviously, size alone does not define world class since many large firms grow to be among the largest corporations in the world and then lose their footing. Perhaps public opinion and corporate reputation play a role in being perceived as world class.

In teaching executive education workshops for two decades, I have asked the class participants (managers, executives, and professionals) to categorize a list of 10 to 12 companies as winning and losing. Two things commonly happen. First, most groups don't articulate the factors they use to define winning and losing, although there is almost always a tacit expectation of current revenue and stock performance. Second, some companies (such as Apple, Dell, and Starbucks) have floated between the two columns, depending on the year. The executives' gut instinct is to define winning or losing in the short term even though in further discussion they define a true winner, a successful world-class company, as managing itself for the long term. Winning companies should be healthy companies. Competitive advantages are fleeting, and companies must continue to find new ones. IBM, for example, celebrated its centennial in 2011—and it's a very different company than it was when it started. Its **centennial video** demonstrates its ongoing business

http://www.youtube.com/watch?v=39jtNUGgmd4

renewal.

Let's use a different lens: admiration rankings. *Fortune*'s surveys of the most admired companies have yielded dramatically different results between 1984 and 2011. To gather the results, *Fortune* commissioned the Hay Group to survey executives, directors, and securities analysts to select top companies on the basis of innovation, people management, financial soundness, quality of management, use of corporate assets, social responsibility, long-term investments, and quality of products and services. Each

Table 1-2

Fortune's Top 10 Most Admired Companies

	1984	2011
1	IBM	Apple
2	Dow Jones	Google
3	Hewlett-Packard	Berkshire Hathaway
4	Merck	Southwest Airlines
5	Johnson & Johnson	Procter & Gamble
6	Time, Inc.	Coca-Cola
7	General Electric	Amazon.com
8	Anheuser-Busch	FedEx
9	Coca-Cola	Microsoft
10	Boeing	McDonald's

of these criteria might spawn what are perceived to be best practices. Here again we see different companies moving on and off the list over time (Table 1-2).

Thus, it's more than stock value and admiration scores. Perhaps we must look at the underlying health of a firm: its ability to improve and sustain performance in the future. What are the elements of a healthy company? Different metrics are appropriate for different industries and situations. Although we occasionally read about centenarians living a long life despite not taking care of themselves, that is the exception rather than the rule. Some activities that feel good in the short term may be hazardous in the long term. We can list at least a few factors related to longevity, such as exercise, a good diet, and efforts to maintain health. The same thing is true of companies. Successful short-term performance occasionally comes at the expense of underlying health. Thus, there are many definitions of winning and losing, as evidenced by the various rankings in Tables 1-3 and 1-4.

One of the potential problems of blindly following world-class principles is that companies begin to benchmark themselves against leaders in the existing industry (this is sometimes a risk with Porter's five forces analysis). Over time these companies may begin to perform at a higher level than the market leader and drift toward complacency. To challenge your own complacency, study the practices of niche players or others that may change the rules in the future. Don't allow benchmarking to cause complacency. Expecting simply to fill out templates and implement best practices abdicates the role of leadership.

Table 1-3

Winning or Losing? Company Comparisons on Various Rankings

Company	Fortune 500	Most Admired	Top Global Brands	Best to Work For	Customer Service Champs
Walmart	1	11			
GE	6	13	5		
Coca-Cola	70	6	1		
IBM	18	12	2		
Starbucks	229	16	97	98	*
Apple	35	1	17		
Microsoft	38	9	3	72	
AT&T	12				
Toyota		33	11		
Dell	41		35		

*Received an honorable mention since there were no other restaurants to compare it against.

Fortune 500, *Fortune* May 23, 2011. Lists the largest corporations in terms of revenues. Included in the survey are U.S. incorporated companies filing financial statements with a government agency.

Most Admired, *Fortune* March 21, 2011 (ranks only top 50). Hay Group surveyed 3,322 executives, directors, and securities analysts to select top companies on the basis of innovation, people management, financial soundness, quality of management, use of corporate assets, social responsibility, long-term investment, and quality of products and services.

Top Global Brands, Interbrand website, November 11, 2010. Interbrand evaluates brand value on the basis of how much it is likely to earn for the company in the future, using analysts' projections, company financial documents, and its own analysis to arrive at a net present value of those earnings. At least a third of the earnings must be from outside the firm's home country. Rankings are based on the net present value calculation.

Best to Work For, *Fortune*, February 7, 2011. *Fortune* surveyed nearly 100,000 employees to pick the winners.

Customer Service Champs, *BusinessWeek*, March 25, 2011. Uses a combination of JDPower data and surveys to evaluate perceived quality of staff and quality of service, with staff weighted at 60 percent and service efficiency (processes) at 40 percent. The results are provided on J.D. Power's website rather than in print publication.

Table 1-4

Top 20 Companies in Each List

Rank	**Fortune 500** May 23, 2011	**Most Admired** March 21, 2011	**Top Global Brands** November 11, 2010	**Best to Work For** February 7, 2011	**Customer Service Champs** March 25, 2011
1	Walmart	Apple	Coca-Cola	SAS	Amazon.com
2	Exxon Mobil	Google	IBM	Boston Consulting Group	USAA
3	Chevron	Berkshire Hathaway	Microsoft	Wegmans Food Markets	Jaguar
4	ConocoPhillips	Southwest Airlines	Google	Google	Lexus
5	Fannie Mae	Procter & Gamble	GE	NetApp	The Ritz-Carlton
6	General Electric	Coca-Cola	McDonald's	Zappos	Publix
7	Berkshire Hathaway	Amazon.com	Intel	Camden Property Trust	Zappos.com
8	General Motors	FedEx	Nokia	Nugget Market	Hewlett-Packard
9	Bank of America	Microsoft	Disney	REI	T. Rowe Price
10	Ford Motor	McDonald's	Hewlett-Packard	Dreamworks Animation SKG	Ace Hardware
11	Hewlett-Packard	Walmart	Toyota	Edward Jones	Keybank
12	AT&T	IBM	Mercedes-Benz	Scottrade	Four Seasons Hotels and Resorts
13	JPMorgan Chase & Co.	General Electric	Gillette	Alston & Bird	Nordstrom
14	Citigroup	Walt Disney	Cisco	Robert W. Baird & Co.	Cadillac
15	McKesson	3M	BMW	Mercedes-Benz	Amica
16	Verizon Communications	Starbucks	Louis Vuitton	JM Family Enterprises	Enterprise Rent-a-Car
17	American International Group	Johnson & Johnson	Apple	USAA	American Express
18	IBM	Singapore Airlines	Marlboro	Stew Leonard's	Trader Joe's
19	Cardinal Health	BMW	Samsung	Methodist Hospital System	JetBlue Airways
20	Freddie Mac	American Express	Honda	Cisco	Apple

ARE THERE BEST-PRACTICE BUSINESS MODELS?

A *best practice*, as defined by Wikipedia, is "a technique, method, process, activity, incentive, or reward that is believed to be more effective at delivering a particular outcome than any other technique, method, process, etc." That's a very broad statement, but many managers seem to believe that there is a magic bullet in the form of world-class processes and best practices that you can plug in to your firm and guarantee success. Unfortunately, it's not that easy. Business success requires hard work, resources, and often plain luck. I read on a blog somewhere that best practices come from practicing your best consistently. That's not a bad idea. Perhaps future best practices will be those which turn conventional wisdom upside down.

We can find several examples of what happens with the overuse of best practices. Long before Google became noted for allowing its engineers to pursue pet projects, 3M encouraged researchers to spend unscripted time exploring potential new products. Between 2001 and 2005, when former GE executive James McNerney was CEO of 3M, emphasis shifted to operational efficiency and the application of Six Sigma techniques. Although waste was curbed and margins improved in the short term, it took a toll on the 3M business model of innovation. Six Sigma is still important in 3M's factories, but not in its labs.

A growth agenda is typically part of a firm's strategy, which by definition is a long-term plan of action to achieve a particular goal. Several authors have attempted to define the management practices that are linked to successful performance (most commonly defined as long-term stock performance). Nitin Nohria in an article in *Harvard Business Review* titled "What Really Works" studied 160 companies over a 10-year period and identified four primary management practices: strategy, execution, culture, and structure. It's worth noting that the authors did not define best practices in these four areas but suggested that superior performance came from clarity and alignment of these variables.

A few years later Christian Stadler in "The 4 Principles of Enduring Success" in *Harvard Business Review* reported on a 50-year benchmarking study of European companies. The principles identified included the following: (1) exploit existing assets before exploring new ones, (2) diversify the business portfolio to gain economies of scope, (3) learn from mistakes, and (4) be conservative about change. These two articles define success from the perspective of stock performance. In light of possible changes in the stock market, this definition of success might morph. As of 2011, Facebook and Twitter were avoiding public markets by raising millions or billions of dollars privately, although by the end of 2011 Facebook was considering going public. Even Apple and Google, which have a market presence, are not paying dividends in the way prior generation companies did. Whether these examples change capitalistic business models is yet to be seen.

As was suggested above, rather than detailed best practices, success comes from thoughtful analysis and interpretation of information. In fact, sometimes taking the opposite approach can be the best thing to do. Rather than learning from best practices, can you learn more from worst practices and failures?

Sometimes disruptions are so obvious that we can't overlook them, and at other times they sneak up on us. That's why it is important to review your business model as often as you review your strategy. Sometimes a change in strategy is sufficient to make progress toward your goals, sometimes a major restructuring of your business model is necessary, and in some situations a strategy change morphs into a business model change.

Michael Malone in *The Future Arrived Yesterday: The Rise of the Protean Corporation and What It Means for You* argues that companies in the future will need to be "shape-shifters" that reinvent themselves on an ongoing basis. The causes for this are multiple. Ubiquitous technology, a global economy, and "networks of free agents" are all contributors to the need for ongoing reincarnations. The major challenge will be to determine how to couple permanence with perpetual change.

Alexander Osterwalder and Yves Pigneur in *Business Model Generation*

http://www.youtube.com/watch?v=sKvKQf4-EGM

recommend that organizational leaders analyze and discuss nine business model building blocks: customer segments, value propositions, channels, customer relationships, revenue streams, key resources, key activities, key partnerships, and cost structure. They recommend a simple approach of plotting the building blocks on a poster and using Post-it notes to describe how each one is related to a firm's business model and what might need to change. New business models may emerge from different combinations of variables.

Mark Johnson in *Seizing the White Space* has reduced this set of factors

http://www.youtube.com/watch?v=Ygc_Q8GkBLk

into four elements, which he calls "the four-box framework": customer value proposition, key resources, key processes, and profit formula. His approach is to encourage managers to define potentially new business models by exploring the complex interdependencies of these parts.

The authors of both books identified the following categories of business models (with examples of each in parentheses). Osterwalder and Pigneur describe five patterns: unbundling models (private banking), the long tail (LEGO), multisided platforms (Google), free (Skype), and open business models (Procter & Gamble). Johnson's archetypal examples included high-cost solution shop (system integrators), high-volume value-adding process businesses (MinuteClinic), and democratized facilitated networks (online auctions).

ESTABLISH A PLANNING FRAMEWORK

Let's take a look at how all of these items work together in a business model planning framework, starting with general strategy principles (see Figure 1-1). Strategic planning is a management tool, a disciplined effort to produce fundamental decisions and actions, and many of the principles are components of business model renewal. The internal and external scan [often referred to as strengths, weaknesses, opportunities, threats (SWOT)] analysis helps shape the mission, vision, and business model of an organization. The mission, vision. and values (MVV) help assess the relevance of the factors evaluated in the scan. Note that the scan and the MVV are tools rather than substitutes for the exercise of judgment by a firm's leaders. The leadership uses all that information to assess the perceived readiness of an organization to make a strategic change as well as to make specific decisions on the goals of the strategy.

The level of readiness for organizational change will have an impact on efforts toward business model renewal. There are situations in which circumstances in the environment have become so pressing that the need for change is clear. In those cases leaders can tap into the organization's existing knowledge (and occasionally fear) to help propel efforts in a new direction. In contrast, there are organizations that over the last two decades or

FIGURE 1-1 ➤ Business model planning framework

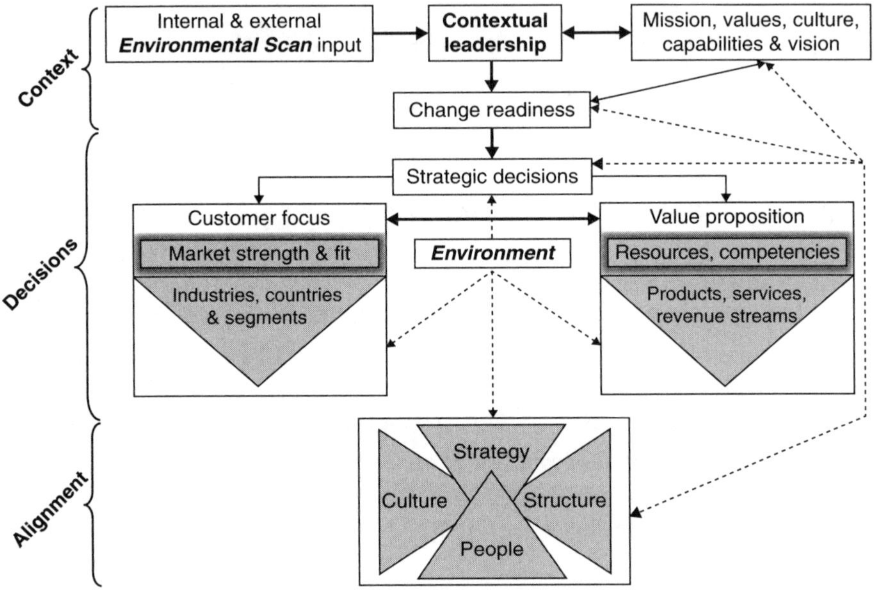

so have begun to develop a more interdependent leadership culture with an organizational mindset built on adaptability. If this type of leadership and organizational culture is already present, new change initiatives will be close to business as usual, creating a more change-ready environment for business model renewal.

However, for a significant number of companies, neither of these two situations exists. In that case it becomes incumbent on the leader to plan up front to build change readiness into the organization as early in the process as possible. If done right, this will force communication across the organization, providing an opportunity to plant seeds for future support and buy-in. It will help minimize the risk of becoming overly optimistic about the time and effort required to move toward a new business model.

There are two fundamental strategic decisions leaders make: who should be the strategic customers (in terms of industries, markets, segments, countries, etc.) and what potential or plausible value proposition will be provided for them (in terms of products, services, solutions, technologies, revenue streams, etc.). These decisions are not separate since value is a by-product of market definition. Adding products (which have related costs) that have no value to customers or prospects is rarely a good strategic decision. (Some exceptions include preparing for a divestiture and taking an advantage of an opportunistic venture that is not inconsistent with the strategy, but those are only rarely the rule.)

The addition of the environment in the dotted area in the figure suggests the importance of being consciously responsive to a dynamic environment in both crafting and implementing strategy. It is not possible simply to create a strategic plan and implement it as is.

Finally, the alignment of strategy, structure, culture, and people establishes the framework of the business model. Note that most of the lines have reciprocal arrows rather than being one-directional. This is due to the fact that strategic planning and business modeling do not flow smoothly from one step to the next. The process is more iterative and creative, inevitably moving back and forth several times as new information is obtained and processed. Strategic leaders continually balance the fit of the strategy with the culture and business model as well as the evolvability of both the strategy and the business model: its ability to evolve as circumstances change.

Note the three domains on the left of the model: Context, Decisions, and Alignment. Leaders obtain the context for planning through the scan and knowledge of the "soul" or culture of the company. Then they make connected decisions about strategic goals. Finally, they ensure alignment of the various components. Each of these domains will be examined below.

DOMAIN 1: CONTEXT

The environmental scanning process involves scanning, monitoring, forecasting, and assessing data about the firm as well as the external environment in which it exists. This is the time for executives to immerse themselves in information, to temporarily allow chaos to reign before trying to rein in the chaos. SWOT, as discussed above, stands for strengths, weaknesses, opportunities, and threats. The strengths and weaknesses are management assessments of internal—and presumably controllable—variables that affect a firm's ability to compete in the future. The opportunities and threats represent the assessment of the external—and uncontrollable—variables that a company must react to or prepare for in developing a strategic (future-focused) plan. Sometimes a strength for one market (or compared with one competitor) can be a weakness for another. Similarly, what is perceived as a threat by one company or individual may be perceived as an opportunity by another. Since there will always be subjective interpretations, it's useful to conduct the SWOT as a cross-functional exercise.

Internal Scan

Starting with strengths, consider the sources of success over the last few years that seem to give you a potentially sustainable advantage in the marketplace for the future:

1. What products or services do you have that are both important to the market and unique or superior to current and potential competition?
2. What successful systems or processes do you own that are difficult for others to copy?
3. What assets (e.g., buildings) or resources (e.g., capital) might provide an edge in the marketplace? (See Table 1-5 for example resources and indicators.)
4. What "soft" assets (e.g., brand equity, human resources, corporate culture) might you be able to capitalize on?
5. What proprietary technology might you be able to leverage?

Some of the strategy approaches that will be mentioned in Chapter 2 have embedded tools to help out with this process. For example, questions posed by the various authors in the "growth from the core" category help a firm determine whether a strength is truly a distinctive competency. Many firms begin their SWOT analysis by listing a bunch of bullet-pointed strengths on a flipchart but do not determine whether these factors are distinctively different from the competition or whether they might establish some future advantage.

When completing the internal scan, be aware of the risk of being overly pessimistic or overly optimistic. In either case companies can become trapped by the images they have of themselves. Pessimism is quite common when a company has been battered by a variety of forces and employees feel there is no hope. As a result true strengths can be downplayed or ignored and despair sets in. Whenever someone highlights what have long been success factors, others may feel compelled to think about the negatives. "But all of our competitors have that exact strength." "But we tried exploiting those strengths and continue to be unsuccessful." "But we have no budget to compete effectively." If the internal evaluation devolves in this way, ask yourself if your "but" is too big! And then shift toward the positive.

On the other hand, unrealistic optimism can be just as treacherous—especially when employees are in denial regarding obsolescence of products, processes, or skills and become cavalier about claiming superiority. When do the organizational competencies that caused your firm's success become impediments to situational response or growth? Think beyond strengths as they *are* to also consider strengths as they might *be leveraged* to truly confer unique benefits and contribute to your firm's advantage. Test your thinking before pinning your future successes on perceived strengths.

Table 1-5

Assets and Resources

RESOURCE	MAIN CHARACTERISTICS	KEY INDICATORS
Tangible resources		
Financial resources	The firm's borrowing capacity and its internal funds generation determine its capacity for investment expenditure and ability to weather fluctuations in demand and profits over time	Debt-to-equity ratio Ratio of net cash to capital expenditures Credit rating
Physical resources	The size, location, technical sophistication, and flexibility of plant and equipment Location and alternative uses for land and buildings Reserves of raw materials Physical resources constrain the firm's set of production possibilities and determine important aspects of the firm's cost position	Resale values of fixed assets Age of capital equipment Scale of plants Flexibility of plant and equipment
Intangible resources		
Technological resources	*Stock of technology* in the form of proprietary technology (patents, copyright, trade secrets) and expertise in the application of technology (know-how) *Resources for innovation*: research facilities, technical and scientific employees	Number and significance of patents Revenue from patent licenses R&D staff as a percentage of total employment
Reputation	Reputation with customers through the ownership of brands, established relationships with customers, the reputation of the firm's products and services for quality, reliability, etc.; the reputation of the company with suppliers (including the component suppliers, banks and other lenders, employees and potential employees), with the government and government agencies, and with the community.	Brand recognition Price premium over competing brands Percentage of repeat buying Level and consistency of company performance Objective measures of product performance
Human resources	The *training and expertise* of employees determine the skills available to the firm; the *adaptability of employees* determines key aspects of strategic flexibility of the firm The *commitment and loyalty* of employees determines the capacity of the firm to attain and maintain competitive advantage	Educational, technical, and professional qualifications of employees Compensation relative to industry Record of labor disputes Employee turnover rate

Source: Robert M. Grant, *Contemporary Strategy Analysis*, Blackwell, 1998, p. 114.

By using a simple acronym such as DIVE, you can evaluate these items more carefully. Is the strength *DURABLE*? Will you be able to benefit from this strength for at least the duration of your defined strategic planning cycle, or is it fleeting? Is the strength *INIMITABLE*? How likely is it that competitors —or noncompetitors—can copy you on this characteristic within this time frame? Can customers find a substitute or provide it themselves? Is the strength *VALUABLE*? Does the strength help you provide a concrete value proposition for your specified target market? Will changes in technology, economics, regulations, or other variables make its value obsolete? Finally, can the strength be *EXPLOITED* in a way that generates profit or value for the firm? Some strengths may satisfy the first three criteria but are invisible to customers, and as a result it is challenging to persuade the customers to pay for the value they are receiving. Alternatively, sometimes a strength is not exploited because it is inconsistent with the culture of the organization. In the final analysis, ask yourself what it is that only your firm can do.

After addressing the five questions related to strengths, it's now time to shift to weaknesses. Look for potential vulnerabilities inside your company that could be an Achilles' heel in the future.

1. Do you lack any critical products, solution components, systems, resources, or assets that could put you at a competitive disadvantage in your marketplace?
2. What gaps or potentially obsolescent capabilities and competences exist in your firm?
3. Are you lacking any strengths compared with the competition?

External Scan

Some companies use generic statements of opportunities and threats (OT) as part of a SWOT analysis for the external scan, but it is useful to incorporate more questions. Start with the TIME acronym (Figure 1-2), using a combination of factual data and intuition to arrive at broad ideas.

Technology

Technology trends can provide opportunities for organizations to improve operational efficiency, create new products, or interact more effectively with customers. Improvements in hardware and software in information technology (IT) have provided data warehouses for knowledge industries, factory automation for manufactured product industries, and GPS tracking for location-based services. Trends in digitization have spawned mobile devices

FIGURE 1-2 ➤ Time categories for external scan

with numerous applications, from cell-phone banking to photo capture (there's an app for that). Other new products resulting from new technologies include hybrid cars, alternative energy, and satellite communications. Finally, customers have begun to interact with firms through blogs, Twitter, and Facebook.

Sometimes technologies from one industry can be adapted for another. RFID (radio frequency identification), for example, increased warehouse efficiency and later was adopted by state highway departments to collect tolls without having drivers stop to pay cash. X-ray technology has shifted from medical applications to security applications (and vice versa). Computer technologies have merged with other electronics to morph into home entertainment.

Think about technology, science, and innovation in your industry and in similar industries:

- Can technologies from other industries be adapted?
- Are novel applications possible?
- Are there any technologies that might improve your efficiency, effectiveness, or long-term advantages if you capitalized on them?
- Are there any technologies that might put your efficiency, effectiveness, or long-term advantages at risk if you ignored them?

- What technological changes are expected or anticipated?
- Are there any technology trends that could make something you do become obsolete?

Industry

An industry is a group of firms that sell similar products or services to essentially the same market. Every industry is composed of buyers, suppliers, and competitors. From an organizational perspective, attractive industries have buyers and suppliers with minimal bargaining strength, few potential substitutes for the product or service being provided, competitors that are unlikely to attack one another aggressively, and a low likelihood of new competitors entering the industry. Unattractive industries have just the opposite. The reality is that industries vary depending on how they are defined (for example, does the healthcare industry include just healthcare providers or also insurers?), and most have a combination of attractive and unattractive components.

The challenge for firms is to identify the unattractive components (the industry's weaknesses) and figure out a way to turn them to their advantage. If the traditional buyers wield significant power, can you redefine the buyer or find segments of buyers with less bargaining strength? For example, Stihl decided to sell its power tools exclusively through dealers rather than big box channels such as Walmart and Home Depot, thus changing its bargaining strength. It also provides a different value proposition for the dealers, which would have been difficult if it had targeted large retailers. Similarly Bright Horizons, an organization that operates daycare facilities within corporate environments as a convenience for the employees, redefined the buyer from individual parents to corporations. Even though corporations had more power relative to the parents, Bright Horizons could offer a unique value proposition of employee benefits, a value that would not be relevant for the traditional buyers. That also redefined the competitors, resulting in less head-to-head competition.

The industry analysis also should include a study of competitor's strengths, weaknesses, and potential strategies. Some companies even conduct war games in which they attempt to think like their competitors to determine how best to position themselves for future success.

Think about your industry. How would you define the industry structure in terms of buyers, suppliers, and competition?

How is your firm uniquely positioned compared with these competitors? What is your value proposition today, and will you be able to maintain it in the future? What challenges might you face?

Who are your suppliers' competitors? Are there any trends that might influence the relationship you have with your existing suppliers? If the relationship changes, how might that affect your long-term strategy?

What is the traditional buyer in the industry? Are there any other buyers to consider for the future?

Market

The market refers to your existing and prospective customers and takes the analysis of the buyer from the industry analysis a bit deeper. Within your existing customer base, there are primary, secondary, and tangential (or possibly opportunistic) clients. If your business ceased to exist, which customers would be most affected? That provides some insight into who your core customers are, and this group may or may not consist of both current and prospective customers.

Think about your core or primary market:

- Is this market stable, growing, or declining?
- Have you saturated this market, or is there room for profitable growth?
- How large is this market and what is the projected growth rate? How might it change in the future?
- For what articulated or unarticulated needs must you prepare?

Are there adjacent markets that offer opportunities for the future?

Are there higher-level sociocultural trends to consider? For example, what impact might trends in each of the following areas have on you? What other areas might be important?

- Lifestyles
- Values
- Leisure
- Demography
- Education
- Health issues

External Events and Trends

This is the infamous "miscellaneous" or "other" category. It includes political, economic, environmental, legal, and other factors that could influence the success of a long-term strategy. Consider both the probability and the strategic impact of an event occurring within your planning cycle (say, three to five years). The greater the probability and the greater the potential impact, the more you will want to build an event into your planning.

Similarly, if a trend is occurring at a specific rate, estimate whether it will continue at that rate for the duration of the planning cycle. Prepare for where that trend might take you by the end of your planning cycle.

Are there existing laws or requirements that pose opportunities or threats?
What pending legislation might affect your future? What should you build into the strategy to prepare for it?
What governmental and political changes might happen, and what might be the consequences?
Might changing public sentiment affect your success?
Are there any lobbying efforts that might change the status quo during your planning cycle?
Are there any environmental, ecological, or sustainability issues to consider?

Porter's Five Forces

http://www.youtube.com/watch?v=mYF2_FBCvXw

Another approach to looking at the industry is to use Michael Porter's five forces analysis, a classic approach that provides a framework for evaluating the attractiveness of an industry (Figure 1-3). It can be useful in diversifying into a new industry, starting a new company, launching a product into a different market, or examining industry factors from the perspective of minimizing negatives and maximizing positives. The ultimate aim of analyzing the structure of an industry is define ways to cope with or change the rules in the firm's favor.

Buyer power, one of the five forces, is determined by the size and impact of customers. Powerful buyers can demand costly service, low prices, and special concessions. The degree of their power depends on several factors. Buyers are powerful if they purchase a significant percentage of the seller's product, especially if it is standardized; if it is easy for them to switch their purchases to the competition (i.e., there are low switching costs); and if buyers pose a credible threat of backward integration. Companies assessing industries with significant buyer power can attempt to redefine the buyer,

FIGURE 1-3 ➤ Porter's five forces

create new segments, provide unique products and services, and/or create switching costs.

Supplier power, a force at the opposite end of the supply chain, is another of the five forces. Powerful suppliers can raise prices on raw materials even if the manufacturing firm is unable to recapture the additional cost downstream with increased prices. Suppliers are powerful if their materials are significant to their customers' businesses, if there are few competing suppliers, and if the cost of switching from them is high. Companies in industries with significant supplier power can attempt to redesign their goods and services to reduce their reliance on the suppliers and/or simplify the cost of switching between suppliers.

The *threat of substitution*, the third force (we are discussing the forces in an order slightly different from that in the figure), generally comes from products and services outside the industry. For example, downloading music onto MP3 players or iPods has replaced purchases of music on CDs at music stores. The more likely it is that new products, services, or technologies can provide the same or similar functionalities as existing offerings, the greater the threat of substitutes is. There are a few different approaches companies facing this type of threat could consider. First, they might focus on niches where their current offering (perhaps as a result of inertia or other factors) is likely to be preferred over the substitutes, such as seniors preferring to use bank tellers rather than use online banking. Second, they might try to find uses for their competencies in other industries, such as clay sewer pipe manufacturers faced with obsolescence by competition from plastic pipes shifting to manufacturing chimney flue liners. Third, they might decide to reinvent their competencies to compete head-on with the substitute products.

The *threat of new competitors* depends partly on the barriers to entry in the industry. It is difficult for new competitors to enter an industry when significant capital is required, access to distribution channels is limited, patents and proprietary knowledge restrict entry, minimum economies of scale are required to be profitable, or there are other absolute cost barriers. If there are few entry barriers, the industry may approach pure competition, in which new competitors can change the rules at any time. Here companies must be aware of price wars as new companies try to gain business from existing players. However, strong entry barriers often imply strong exit barriers as well, meaning that companies may choose to cut prices to enable them to utilize their capacity efficiently.

All these forces together combine to influence the *intensity of competitive rivalry*, the fifth force. Rivalry depends on the number and strength of companies competing for the same customers and resources as well as the presence of switching costs, entry and exit barriers, the industry growth rate, and the potential for overcapacity. Companies in an industry in which competitive intensity is intense may strive to carve out a niche where competition is less severe. If they choose the broad market rather than a niche, they will need to understand the rules to avoid destabilizing the industry into a price war. In other words, they will have to determine the respective positions of the market leaders, the challengers, and the followers.

The role of the contextual leader in domain 1 is to encourage new insights, be open to unexpected interpretations of data, become a role model, set the stage for the urgency to act, and prepare to engage the pertinent team in the organization. Leaders at all levels of the organization will have to participate in the effort to respond to the current-day context for their organization while simultaneously planning for the future.

Leaders sometimes need to forget parts of the past in an effort to create the future. This is challenging since planning processes, performance evaluation systems, incentives, organizational structures, and company policies are based on the existing way of doing business.

Domain 1 is not a singular event or even a series of concrete steps. Rather, it's an iterative process of exploration, unfreezing, relearning, and challenging norms and assumptions.

It's more than seeking best practices. Successful leaders certainly don't ignore contemporary hot topics. However, they go beyond simply learning them to adapting them actively to the needs of their businesses at a specific point in time. A strategy of efficiency, for example, is most effective when the business model and customer value proposition are on target. Although defects are never desired, the reality is that customers probably won't care about defects if they don't want the product in the first place. Although all these ideas are pieces to a puzzle (or sometimes pieces to different puzzles), individual managers and leaders must accept the fact that they are simply tools to provide the context for decisions. They do not provide answers.

DOMAIN 2: STRATEGIC DECISIONS

As leaders gain knowledge of the context described above, they apply that knowledge to decision making. The decisions revolve around how to create value (through products, services, and revenue streams) as well as for whom those offerings actually have value. Chapter 2 addresses three broad categories of growth that result from the intersections of these decision variables: sustaining, transformative, and disruptive growth. Although there's nothing magic about these categories, they can be used to promote thinking from a portfolio perspective. Chapters 3 through 5 on foresight, innovation, and decision making provide mental models and tools to help you escape short-term myopia as you make the strategic decisions of domain 2.

DOMAIN 3: ALIGNMENT

Leadership has to continue from context to decisions and finally to alignment. Apple often is identified as a company to learn from when it comes to effective strategy execution. Yet even Apple has experienced failures as well as successes. The commercial launch of the iPad was considered by Schneider & Associates to be the most memorable of 2010. However, this was not Apple's first entry into the tablet market. The Newton emerged in the early 1990s, but the complete ecosystem was not yet ready. Similarly, the iPod probably would not have been as successful without the market's experience with other MP3 players, the copyright solutions pushed by issues surrounding Napster, and the improvements in online speed and connectivity. Ron Adner wrote in a 2006 *Harvard Business Review* article that "Apple's brilliance was not in being the *first* to put down a piece of the puzzle, but in being the first to put down the *last* piece of the puzzle." Your challenge is to figure out how to be the first in your market space to put down the last piece of the strategy puzzle and align it with your business model.

Companies with room to grow from the core (sustaining growth) may be able to do so without significant changes to their business models. The more firms require transformative and disruptive growth strategies, the more pressure there will be for business model change. Business models resulting from decisions to create value may look good on paper, but the actual value creation doesn't happen until strategy, structure, culture, and people are aligned. That's the focus of the final section of this book.

KAY PLANTES

THE IMPORTANCE OF DEVELOPING A BUSINESS MODEL PORTFOLIO

Kay Plantes, Ph.D., is an MIT-trained economist and corporate strategy expert who has helped organizations of all sizes, industries, and sectors escape commoditization and achieve ambitious growth goals through business model innovation. Kay is author of *Beyond Price: Differentiate Your Business in Ways That Really Matter* (Greenleaf Book Group, 2009) and a partner in the Agile Strategy Institute. You can read Kay's business model innovation blog at:

http://www.plantescompany.com/blog

Kay Plantes, Ph.D.
Economist, Corporate Strategy Expert, and Author
Plantes Company

***Kay, you are well known as an expert on business models, so I'm going to start with perhaps the most basic of questions. How do you define* business model?**

A business model captures what I call the core strategy decisions of the firm; these are questions that address the design of the business, as opposed to its construction. Simply stated, a business model explains how a company combines resources, processes, and solutions to deliver value to a group of customers with similar needs in return for revenue that not only covers costs but generates a profit for the firm.

There are many different definitions and visual depictions of business models in the literature, defined in part by how the authors go about helping leaders innovate their business models. To me key design decisions of the business model are:

- Target market: how you reach them and develop a relationship with them
- Solutions
- Value promise
- Why your value promise is hard for competitors to copy
- Profit model (revenue model, cost structure, etc.)

Ultimately, it's about how you align resources, processes, and solutions to deliver customer value in return for cash flow and other company stakeholder returns.

Whatever their differences, they each explain how shared value—for the customer and the organization—is created, where value for the customer is, the benefits customers get from an organization's solutions minus the costs they pay to receive these benefits. These costs and benefits can be direct (purchase price, more throughput in the production line) or indirect (time savings, less frustration).

Leaders often forget their Economics 101 principles. Over time, the benefits offered by different competitors become more and more similar, making cost more and more important until price drives customer choice; this is the definition of a commodity market. If you do not have the lowest-cost product, for example, you must deliver benefits that are hard for current or new competitors to copy.

The speed with which product and service commoditization arises in today's more open economy is remarkable. Price transparency, stronger buyers, supply chains that can copy anything, excess supply, the global recession, and slow recovery—there are many forces behind the acceleration. Collectively they are shifting the basis of competition from individual products and services to business models because business models are harder for competitors to copy. I always tell my clients, "Every industry has its Walmart, the lowest-cost business model. If that's not what you want to be or can be, avoid becoming your industry's Sears. Think like Target—build a different business model."

Are there other reasons why the concept of business models has become such an important topic in the business press recently?

Business models are not a new concept; they have been there since the start of barter, the beginning of a more open economy in which there is exchange between two people. In protected markets, every industry had its business model. Take K–12 textbooks. Macmillan and its competitors had the same business model and competed on the same basis: scale (e.g., size of the sales force, run length for printing costs), quality of content, and efficiency. The best executors got the best market share, and there were very few entrants because of the high cost of securing state textbook adoptions that opened doors to school districts buying your curriculum. You needed a large sales force as well as money to create the prototype textbooks and teachers' guides in advance.

Now think about what the Internet has done, giving any student, teacher, principal, and school district access to the world's knowledge. Content is being redefined, there are multiple ways to reach audiences, and the future of Macmillan will depend on its business model(s) and not just its execution against the old business model. How will Macmillan compete, for example, against Khan Academy: free online curriculum, easy access, demonstrated success in creating learning, and backed by billionaire philanthropists?

The entire PK–12 industry will be reinvented in the United States, as it should be, since the industry's results are dismal. Each student's learning needs are unique, yet we have used mass-market teaching approaches to teach to the middle. Beyond the disruption in what the public is funding (charter schools, for example) there will be disruptions in resources, processes, and solutions that go into educating PK–12 students. Teachers will become learning coaches, and the companies able to supply teachers with content and tools that advance each student's learning in ways linked to school district standards will win enormous market share going forward. All of Macmillan's great "history" may in fact become an albatross slowing down its required changes, just as Kodak's film business slowed down its transition to digital photography.

In industry after industry, barriers to entry are melting away, industry boundaries are disappearing, competitive advantages are becoming obsolete as new ones arise, and products and services are easily copied, thanks to supply chains that can re-create anything, seemingly overnight. In these turbulent seas, the most important question leaders can ask is: Do we have the right business models and how must we evolve them?

Many recent articles have talked about companies needing to reinvent themselves after a stall. Do you think it's possible (or advisable) for companies to proactively reinvent themselves in an attempt to prevent a stall?

The head of product development would be deemed a failure if his or her pipeline did not have products at different stages of the pipeline to ensure an ongoing supply of line extensions and new products into the company's markets. The role of the leadership team in today's turbulent markets is to have a rich portfolio of business models at different stages, from embryonic (where the name of the game is experimentation to see what works), to growth (where the name of the game is taking the model to scale), to maturity (where you run the business model for maximum efficiency and cash flow). A company stall is just an indication that the leadership team's portfolio had a lot of gaps.

Regardless of whether changes are reactive or proactive, modifying a business model can be risky. What can companies do to minimize the potential risks accompanying these changes?

The far larger risk is not changing your business models in today's copycat economy. Business model evolution and redesign is to the twenty-first-century economy what quality improvement was to the industrial age: a required leadership skill.

One of my clients was caught in a commoditized industry, selling highly engineered solutions to general contractors. Despite all the knowledge in the customized solution and risk if the solution was wrong, contracts were awarded on price, as there were "enough" qualified competitors. (Remember that it only takes one other qualified solution to end up in a commodity market where price drives purchase decisions.)

I told my client that his firm should become the general contractor as what the firm could uniquely do was far more beneficial to owners and developers than to general contractors. This leader had to risk competing against its current customers to switch to a better business model. I was asking him to leave one trapeze rung to land on another, accepting a pregnant pause in the middle in which you feel like your business, if not your life, is in limbo. But he and I knew he'd end up with a far stronger business model.

We came up with a measured way of making the transition: finding a hidden market to develop the contracting skills, one in which my client could land a job before contractors knew there was a job to be had. The company also fashioned an offering to very large contractors: taking over parts of large-scale developments which the large contactor would prefer not to manage. The company grew from $5 million to over $100 million in a short period of time, with profits rising at an even faster rate.

This leader recognized the reality. He knew he'd never survive in a commoditized business and an industry that probably would be consolidated as the push for better pricing grew stronger. The larger risk was not changing. So he managed the risks of change by using his outstanding management skills.

Your blog contains many examples of business model innovation. Is there one that really stands out for you?

http://www.plantescompany.com/blog

My favorite example of leadership in the open economy of the twenty-first century is Apple. Apple has great business models, for example, for the iPhone and the new iPad. But these great product-business models emerge from an overall company design that produces winning business models. First, leaders understand the value promise behind all Apple offerings: making us less frustrated and more capable of doing what we want within the digital world. "Cool" is just a brand wrapping over all this; the value promise of the brand is less frustration and enhanced results. Apple started this value promise in computers, then moved into music, then phones, and now into multiple aspects of our mobile life. From this perspective, Apple's retail stores are more than a marketing channel strategy. The stores advance Apple's value promise.

Second, Apple has great platforms of knowledge, skills, design approaches, and solutions that are leveraged across all its business models. Here is a company that spends a smaller percentage of its revenue on R&D than other innovative companies, and year after year it reinvents products, if not industries, because it is leveraging these platforms into new business models.

Finally, Apple has built a collaborative culture that will be very hard for competitors to copy and that underlies its advantages. And its business has a strong surrounding ecosystem, by which I am referring to all the application developers that pull through demand for Apple's products and enhance the value of Apple's products.

Compare Apple to Dell, a company whose wealth was created through a business model innovation: customized computers sold directly to businesses. But then Dell did nothing to evolve its business model other than copy its competitors. Is it any wonder that Dell is caught in between IBM and Apple on the high end and low-cost Asian competitors on the low end? Apple usually has more money in the bank than Dell's entire valuation.

The title of one of your recent blog posts was "Wall Street Ruins Many Sound Business Models." Although I encourage everyone to read the entire post, can you summarize it in a few points?

http://www.plantescompany.com/blog/business-model-innovation-best-practices/wall-street-ruins-many-sound-business-models

First, public companies are wasting an enormous amount of management resources to predict and deliver on earnings to the degree of precision that they do. At a time when you need every general manager and executive VP focused on business model evolution, strengthening the company's portfolio of business models and underlying hard-to-copy advantages, and building a strong ecosystem, you've got top-level people rushing around to make sure Wall Street is not disappointed.

Second, companies establish growth targets unrealistic with what their portfolio of business models can create. Rather than be truthful with Wall Street and explain periods of needed investment, leaders milk companies before business models have hit maturity. In failing to invest, is it any wonder why so many jobs have ended up in China and other parts of Asia? Or public companies enter mergers and acquisitions that only worsen the growth challenge in the years ahead, a strategy that our too-big-to-fail banks and pharmaceutical companies adopted? Is it any wonder that banks and other financial institutions took undue risks to make their numbers, creating our global recession?

Or that so many pharmaceutical company sales forces are found guilty of promoting drugs for applications not approved by the FDA? These issues facing our country and companies are symptoms of a lack of investments on the government and company levels that generate long-term economic opportunity.

To secure year-in, year-out consistent performance, leaders must build a rich portfolio of business models, evolve these business models so they remain strong, and then sell off the highly matured business models to make room for investing in emerging ones the way IBM did in selling off its personal computing and other commoditizing hardware businesses to make room for its Smarter Planet service business. Leaders must build platforms that are leveraged by these business models, platforms that both advance efficiency and enable the company to offer its customers hard-to-copy benefits. And leaders must think about how their businesses relate to the external ecosystem of which they are a part, as competition is increasingly between ecosystems—the Microsoft world or Google world—and not just individual companies.

What final words of advice can you offer business executives who are analyzing their business models?

Remember that in today's open economies, great execution is no longer sufficient for survival or success. Great strategy—the design of your business models, company, and ecosystem—is now a necessary ingredient for success and a key to capturing the many wonderful opportunities that today's open markets create. Make design an ongoing process that is separate from the planning work you must also do to make this year's financial targets.

REFERENCES

Adner, Ron, "Match Your Innovation Strategy to Your Innovation Ecosystem," *Harvard Business Review*, April 2006, p. 98.

Bundelman, R. A., and A. S. Grove, "Let Chaos Reign, Then Rein in Chaos—Repeatedly: Managing Strategic Dynamics for Corporate Longevity," *Strategic Management Journal*, October 2007, pp. 965–979.

Fortune magazine website (for historical information of various rankings).
Hof, Robert D., and Michael Arndt, "How to Hit a Moving Target," *BusinessWeek*, August 21, 2006, p. 80.
Johnson, Mark, *Seizing the White Space: Business Model Innovation for Growth and Renewal*, Harvard Business Press, 2010.
Malone, Michael, *The Future Arrived Yesterday: The Rise of the Protean Corporation and What It Means for You*, Crown Business, 2009.
McKee, Steve, *When Growth Stalls: How It Happens, Why You're Stuck, and What to Do About It*, Jossey-Bass, 2009.
Nohria, Nitin, William Joyce, and Bruce Roberson, "What Really Works," *Harvard Business Review*, July 2003, p. 42.
Olson, Matthew, and Derek van Bever, *Stall Points: Most Companies Stop Growing – Yours Doesn't Have To*, Yale University Press, 2008.
Osterwalder, Alexander, and Yves Pigneur, *Business Model Generation*, Wiley, 2010.
Stadler, Christian, "The 4 Principles of Enduring Success," *Harvard Business Review*, July–August 2007, p. 62.
Worthen, Ben, Cari Tuna, and Justin Scheck, "Companies More Prone to Go 'Vertical,'" *Wall Street Journal*, December 1, 2009.

CHAPTER 2

Define a Growth Agenda

In the interview at the end of Chapter 1, Kay Plantes talked about the challenges caused by the Western growth model of too big to fail and made a very interesting point: Leaders must build a rich portfolio of business models so that they remain strong and then sell off the highly matured business models to make room for investing in emerging ones. Thus, the mental model of growth should not be limited to getting bigger for the sake of being bigger. Rather, an organization should practice *smart* growth to remain healthy.

Growth comes in spurts of regenerative growth as overlapping life cycles of products (and business units) require changes in competencies and potentially in business design. Successful growth must take into account the sustainability of that growth. That requires the right mix of leadership, culture, strategic decisions, and structure. Avoid focusing so much on spreadsheets, numbers, rules, forms, procedures, and protocols that you lose sight of people. Remember that people are required for continued growth to happen.

Growth also can be a by-product of "reproduction" (spin-offs), a variation of Kay's comment above. Although most of the discussion in this chapter and in the book as a whole takes a microeconomic perspective, it is worth mentioning this more macrogrowth concept briefly. For a specific company, the growth rate may decline as size increases, but if the company is split into two, the growth rate for each part could grow since each is calculated on a smaller base. Individual market capitalization will be less, but overall economic growth conceivably could be higher. In addition, many small and midsize enterprises (SMEs) find it easier to have a clearer focus on a distinct value proposition than may be likely for a conglomerate. The spin-offs also reduce the restrictions of centralized decision making and promote stronger responsiveness to the environment.

Companies often face a need to rethink growth during economic downshifts, market or product obsolescence, or strategy transformations. Consistent status quo growth rarely can be sustained in perpetuity. Two recent books address the challenge of growth. *Stall Points* by Matthew Olson and Derek van Bever suggests that revenue growth stalls for the vast majority of Fortune 100 companies are due primarily to management decisions. Consequently, those authors recommend "stress-testing" the assumptions that underlie strategies in an effort to avoid myopia. Steve McKee in *When Growth Stalls* also states that stalled growth is the rule rather than the exception. He emphasizes a strong repositioning strategy to turn things around.

BEWARE OF "ONE-PARADIGM" CONSULTANTS (OR MANAGERS)

Stick to the core. Diversify. Practice lean. Reengineer. Innovate. Define brand archetypes. Create self-directed work teams. Empower your employees. Apply Six Sigma.

Buzzwords create excitement. Buzzwords sell books and services. However, buzzwords don't always help companies become successful, especially when their proponents begin to view all problems according to narrow paradigms. Think about that. The word *paradigm* is defined by Dictionary.com as "a set of assumptions, concepts, values, and practices that constitutes a way of viewing reality for the community that shares them, especially in an intellectual discipline." When "gurus" consistently present their trademarked solution as the best (or only) solution, regardless of the problem in front of them, they are being driven by their paradigm.

Companies have used many different strategies and business models as their road maps for becoming world class. Different orientations have moved in and out of vogue over the years. As I mentioned in the prologue, the simplest definition of a strategy is a long-term plan of action to achieve a particular goal. Using that definition, it's clear that strategies can be developed for athletic teams, products and services, individuals, lines of business, and corporations. I augment that definition to make the link to (and difference from) business models more concrete:

> *Strategy is the art and science of sustaining competitively superior customer value through the most appropriate utilization of resources and assets. It starts with an internal and external scan, then requires leadership in defining a company's future direction, making trade-offs, and structuring an implementation plan.*

Let's look at the different ways academics, consultants and experts have contributed to the ongoing evolution of strategy and business model concepts. I've collapsed the ideas into four buckets:

- Growth from the core
- Pursuit of quality/efficiency advantage
- Pursuit of marketplace advantage
- Innovating into new areas

Growth from the Core

http://www.youtube.com/watch?v=3tfW1iL8uzc

Many experts have described various aspects of a company's core: core philosophies, core business, core ideologies, or core competencies. Tom Peters and Robert Waterman in their *In Search of Excellence* championed the internal cultural philosophies they claimed were the foundation of excellent companies. Among the eight themes they addressed, an important one was "stick to your knitting" (i.e., stay in the business you know well and learn from your customers). Chris Zook and James Allen in *Profit from the Core* presented a similar concept and linked it to marketplace advantage. They encouraged companies to grow from their core, which they defined as "that set of products, customer segments and technologies with which you can build the greatest competitive advantage."

Jim Collins and Jerry Porras in *Built to Last* took a different spin on the concept of core. They encouraged companies to progress toward BHAGs (big, hairy, audacious goals) that built on their core ideologies. They stressed the importance of a core culture that is visionary, with strong ideological values.

It is worth noting that the concept of improving organizational performance by aligning it with tangible goals and vision was introduced by Peter Drucker over a half century ago. His system of management by objectives (MBOs) codified the best practice of strategically aligned goals. When they introduced the balanced scorecard in the 1990s, Kaplan and Norton expanded the concept of goal alignment and measurement so that it became more explicit. Specifically, they proposed the importance of going beyond simple financial goals and objectives to link customer satisfaction, internal processes, and learning and innovation goals to vision and strategy.

Another aspect of core is the set of corporate competencies. C. K. Prahalad and Gary Hamel introduced this concept in their *Harvard Business Review* article "The Core Competence of the Corporation" (May–June 1990). They viewed core competencies as collective learnings (such as production skills and capabilities) in an organization. In the article they suggested that world-class leadership in specific categories of product offerings comes from strengthening core competencies. Other experts, such as George Stalk in "Competing on Capabilities" (*Harvard Business Review*, March–April 1992) and David Collis and Cynthia Montgomery in "Competing on Resources" (*Harvard Business Review,* July–August 1995), expanded the definition of competence to include business capabilities, assets, and both tangible and intangible resources.

Pursuit of Quality/Efficiency Advantage

Another approach companies take to become world class in an increasingly global and competitive marketplace is to apply quality and efficiency tools such as total quality management (TQM), lean, and Six Sigma. There are many similarities across these three methodologies, which all attempt to improve quality by minimizing waste and reducing defects while improving customer satisfaction. However, there are some variations in interpretation and definition.

Total quality management emerged as a significant discipline in the quality movement in Japan after World War II. It became popular in the United States in the 1980s and 1990s as companies in some industries faced loss of world-class status to foreign competitors. W. Edwards Deming, an American statistician, is credited with being the father of the modern quality movement. Wikipedia defines TQM as "a business management strategy aimed at embedding awareness of quality in all organizational processes." In most cases the goal is to define tools and implement a systematic approach to continuously refine processes that both improve bottom-line performance and increase customer satisfaction.

Whether TQM morphed into and was replaced by lean and Six Sigma or whether the three variations have always coexisted is open to debate. However, the latter two are more project- and program-based than TQM. Motorola is recognized as a pioneer in Six Sigma, a practice used to reduce variability and the causes of defects in manufacturing and business processes. *Best practices* embody statistical quality improvement tools along with an infrastructure of champions and various belt levels up to master black belts.

The lean concept, introduced by Toyota, is a variation within the quality movement in which the emphasis is on improving the flow of work and thereby reducing waste. Value stream mapping, 5S, kanban, and just-in-time (JIT) are commonly used tools of this philosophy.

Moving beyond process improvement, the concept of process *reengineering* was championed by Michael Hammer and James Champy in *Reengineering the Corporation*. They recommended evaluating processes from a clean slate in an effort to obliterate non-value-adding work. Whereas TQM espoused continuous improvement, business process reengineering (BPR) sought radical change.

A survey by Maurice Pillet and Jean-Luc Maire in *TQM Journal* confirms "the difficulty companies have in sustaining their improvement processes over time, since the average sustainability ratio for all the different processes [Six Sigma, 5S, BPR, etc.] rarely exceeds 40%." In other words, the more efficient a company gets at a particular process, the harder it is to continue to improve.

Companies also attempt to gain efficiency through vertical integration, on the one hand, or outsourcing, on the other hand. Vertical integration, the argument goes, enables a company to have more complete control of its supply chain and potentially improve its ability to manage the solutions provided to customers. Of course outsourcing, in contrast, enables a firm to devote effort more fully to its core by purchasing rather than internally developing services beyond its core. The pendulum swings from one side to the other over time. Which is better? It depends on the circumstances.

The tools described in this section are appropriate to help implement, for example, the strategy of operational efficiency described in Treacy and Wiersema's *The Discipline of Market Leaders*. However, they may be less useful when various disruptions demand innovation and new business models.

Pursuit of Marketplace Advantage

Some of the earliest attempts to improve strategy started with the SWOT analyses defined by Kenneth R. Andrews in his 1971 book *The Concept of Corporate Strategy*. Companies were encouraged to evaluate their internal strengths and weaknesses (SW) and decide how to use them to gain advantage in light of the opportunities and threats (OT) that existed in the external environment. **Michael Porter** added more discipline to the industry-level analysis of

http://www.youtube.com/watch?v=ibrxIPOH84M

OT with his five forces. The Porter analysis became the gold standard in the 1980s for structural analysis of industries. By examining the bargaining power of buyers and suppliers, along with the intensity of competition from existing competitors, new entrants, and substitutes (i.e., the five forces), companies could determine the potential profitability of industries they might choose to enter. Porter and others (e.g., George Day in *Market-Driven Strategy*) also suggested that the analysis could help in deciding where and how to compete.

Porter elaborated on the concept of marketplace advantage by introducing three generic strategies: cost leadership, differentiation, and focus. With a cost leadership strategy, a firm sets out to reduce the costs associated with creating, producing, and delivering products so that it creates a price advantage in the marketplace (e.g., the Walmart position). Companies that follow a differentiation strategy look for attributes of uniqueness to build into and execute through their business model; the differentiators can be superior products, unmatched services, or dramatically improved solutions. Finally, a focus strategy implies an exceptional concentration on specific market segments and niches; the customer knowledge and relationships emanating from this concentration enable a firm to offer products and services with a superior connection to customer goals and needs.

Michael Treacy and Fred Wiersema provided similar advice in *The Discipline of Market Leaders.* They recommended that companies choose one of three fundamental business strategies: operational excellence, product leadership, and customer intimacy. Companies use an operational excellence strategy when the goal is lower cost and improved efficiency. A product leadership strategy requires continued innovation and market exploration. With a customer intimacy strategy, companies embrace and nurture long-lasting client relationships. The implicit assumption is that the resources required to execute each of these strategies (i.e., the business model) may be significantly different and possibly render them mutually exclusive at times.

Innovating into New Areas

Six Sigma and similar techniques seem to have the most dramatic impact when there is substantial environmental certainty in the product and service areas of an organization. Innovation and reconstruction strategies are used by firms in more rapidly changing environments or when change is necessary for success or even survival. This can be done by creating new markets or by anticipating disruption (estimating when an emerging trend will take off) and building a strategy to take advantage of it.

According to W. Chan Kim and Renee Mauborgne in ***Blue Ocean Strategy***, companies must go beyond competitive advantage in existing markets and create

http://www.youtube.com/watch?v=Qj4vBCadjLw&feature=fvsr

value in new markets to be successful. They argue that industry boundaries are not predetermined and that companies can find uncontested market space that makes competition irrelevant. A primary tool provided in the book is a set of analytical questions called the four actions framework that can be used to look for industry or business model factors to create, eliminate, increase, or decrease.

Rita Gunther McGrath and Ian MacMillan provided similar advice on upending competition in *MarketBusters*. The theme of both books is to look for unserved or underserved segments in which there is an opportunity to create value that doesn't currently exist. Sometimes this can be done with a firm's existing resources, but at other times it may be necessary to modify the business model by building in new competencies.

These two books highlight company-initiated moves, but sometimes entire industries are disrupted and companies must respond. This is where anticipatory innovation comes into play. Companies need to estimate when a radical change might upset the status quo in an industry. For example, digital photography disrupted the film photography industry. Desktop publishing has disrupted traditional publishing. Wireless communications are disrupting wired communications.

Clayton Christensen in *The Innovator's Dilemma* stated that many incumbent leaders in an industry become complacent and are caught off guard when new entrants change the rules as a result of disruptions. In his related book with Michael Raynor, *The Innovator's Solution*, Christensen encourages companies to become disrupters by creating or acquiring the capabilities required for **disrupted growth.** If there was a need to maintain both the existing and

http://www.youtube.com/watch?v=9L66OH-x7a4&NR=1

the new business models, Christensen proposed establishing two separate, distinct organizations, an approach he referred to as the "innovator's solution."

Malcolm Gladwell approached disruption from a different angle in *The Tipping Point*. Dictionary.com defines a tipping point as "the culmination of a build-up of small changes that effects a big change." Gladwell considered a tipping point to be a threshold at which change becomes unstoppable. Although predicting tipping points is an inexact science, companies should monitor trends and experiment with small-scale concepts, strategies, and business models continually.

Although there is significant overlap—and a common goal of competitive advantage—in all these philosophies, the emphases are slightly different.

The first category focuses on exploiting your core business (by emphasizing your strengths) before moving into new market arenas. The second attempts to provide tools to fine-tune your strengths by eliminating flaws. The third brings in the theme of assessing the environment for potential opportunities. The fourth category deals with rethinking opportunities from both disruptive and incremental perspectives.

Eric Abrahamson introduced the concept of *dynamic stability* in strategy, using a series of small-scale experiments, a process he referred to as tinkering and kludging. Michael Treacy, in his work after *The Discipline of Market Leaders*, emphasized ongoing testing and refinement of growth initiatives from existing customers and adjacent markets. Success requires a unique blend of many or all of these philosophies.

THE GROWTH PORTFOLIO

Let us go back to the critical questions in domain 2 of the framework in Chapter 1 and weave in many of the thought processes covered in this chapter. The first question is whether there is room for additional value creation in your current markets as you define them. If the answer is yes, ask whether you can create this value with your current competencies or if a more significant transformation is necessary. A yes to both (as shown in the upper left-hand cell of the growth portfolio model in Figure 2-1) suggests that there is room for sustaining growth. If the answer is no to one or both questions, growth in other areas of the matrix will have to be explored.

FIGURE 2-1 ➤ The growth portfolio

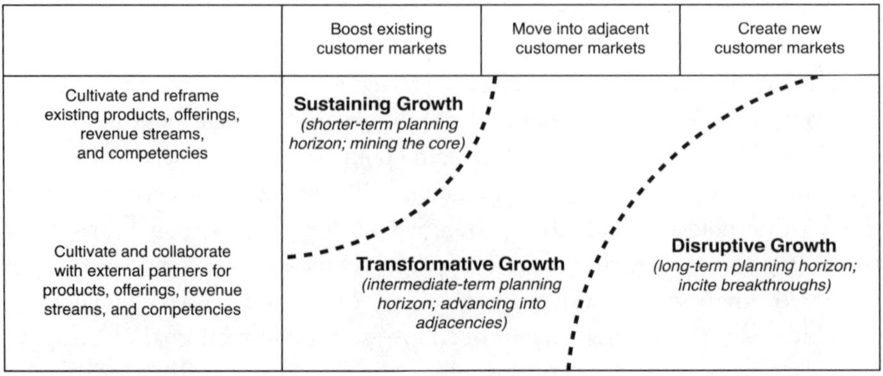

3M CEO George Buckley has laid out goals for that company that seem to mirror these categories: protect and strengthen core businesses (sustaining growth), develop lower-cost products for emerging markets (transformative growth), and explore future opportunities in potential growth markets such as renewable energy (disruptive growth). His goals move the company from the core segment in the upper left to a portfolio of business models across the remaining categories.

My goal is not necessarily to have executives try to plug renewal projects into one of these three buckets. Rather, I'm presenting them as another tool to jump-start thinking from a portfolio mindset and to think about growth from both an external perspective and an internal perspective. (As an aside, I also eliminated the square boxes in the center of the matrix to avoid the mental equivalent of being boxed in.)

Ideas for sustaining growth can come from traditional research and strategic ideation. Transformative growth might build from open innovation and other techniques discussed in Chapter 4. Scenario planning and similar mental models (Chapter 3), along with futuristic approaches to innovation, will be required to generate truly disruptive growth. In terms of time allocations, sustaining growth should be a continuous process. The more companies can continue to build and maintain superior customer loyalty among a well-defined set of customers, the greater their chances of developing a strong market position will be. Also, it's important to avoid ignoring your core business as you expand into new growth arenas. However, as the rate of change in many industries continues to increase, it would be highly risky not to explore transformative and disruptive growth options simultaneously. It's worth noting that although sustaining growth may not require a change in business models, most transformative and disruptive growth initiatives will. It is advisable to establish multifunctional new-growth teams that are small and nimble but also contain seasoned members. These teams can begin to identify and prioritize potential growth initiatives.

I really want to emphasize the wisdom of *and*: the fact that these are not either-or decisions. As Bob Arzbaecher, chairman and CEO of Actuant, states in his end-of-chapter interview, it's possible that continuous incremental innovations over time will result in transformational innovations. When you look back from the future, sustaining growth just might look like major disruptive changes.

SUSTAINING GROWTH

Sustaining growth usually comes from organic growth from the core, such as introducing new products and services for existing customers, selling your

FIGURE 2-2 ➤ Product life cycle decision model

	Reinforce	Renew	Relaunch	Retire
% contribution to profits	high	mid to high	potential	low
Brand value	high	potentially high	potentially high	declining
Strategic fit	solid	can be grown	can be grown	declining
Growability	self-sustaining	growable	growable	unsustainable
Time-based potential	solid current	future growth potential	future growth potential	past performer
Strategy and resource commitment	maintain: focused and steady resources	grow: increase resource commitment	grow: burst of supporting resources	contract: reduce support

current products to different customer segments, dominating channel and support services, and renewing or extending product life cycles. But it's important to do this from the perspective of solving customer needs better than anyone else. The initiatives in this area focus on creating new or more customer value without significant changes in strategy, structure, culture, or business models. This may include making decisions on whether to protect and maintain core products, services, or revenue streams; renew underperformers; retire end-of-life offerings; and resurrect or relaunch concepts and products that may have a chance for a second life. Some points to consider in making these decisions are listed in the product life cycle decision model (Figure 2-2).

Reinforcement and Protection Strategies

A reinforcement product (or service or business unit) generates a good income stream but may not require significant marketing or operational expenditures. It may be a secondary product that doesn't face much competitive pressure, or it may be a core product that has strong brand equity. In either case, look for ways to continue to create value with minimal cost outlays.

Reinforcement strategies are primarily defensive or self-sustaining in nature, attempting to prevent loss to the competition and/or prolong a revenue stream. They can be applied to core products, fillers, or ancillary products. Maintenance strategies should require minimal oversight to free up time—and possibly resources—to devote to revitalizing other products or innovating new offerings and business models. Common examples of maintenance strategies are (1) stay the course, (2) reduce the scope, and (3) defend the perimeter.

Stay the Course

Some products are perennially under the radar, supported by die-hard customers. They don't require much push because of the limited competition. Local breweries, for example, retain their uniqueness by sticking to limited production of beer. Growth beyond this level would entice new competition and potentially make profitable growth more difficult.

Reduce the Scope

Sometimes a product that otherwise might have been eliminated can be maintained by scaling back and focusing on a smaller niche market. This was the case with the Fisher Space Pen, better known as the astronaut pen. The growing economy in the 1990s provided the perfect environment for little indulgences such as a $50 pen that writes under extreme conditions, especially after it was featured on a *Seinfeld* episode. Unfortunately, the downturn in the economy in the early 2000s abruptly lessened demand for the product. The only way to maintain sales was to focus on the truly core users: the "extreme professionals" in "extreme jobs." For example, police officers could use them to write vital signs on latex gloves at accident scenes. Therefore, the target customers for the product shifted to nurses, police, and paramedics.

Defend the Perimeter

A danger in taking your eye off a core business is that competitors can begin to nibble around the edges, a phenomenon also referred to as ankle biting. Therefore, some efforts have to be made to protect against competitive threats by retaining visibility in front of the customer while still squeezing every dollar out of your operating expenditures. Although a disproportionate amount of funds may be invested to launch a product, a smaller amount could be spent on reminder sales promotions once loyalists have been established in the customer base.

Renewal and Revitalization Strategies

Renewal products require revitalization; they can be at any stage of the product life cycle but are not performing at a level objectively determined to be possible. These products require specific demand creation activities to gain increased use or market penetration. There are several approaches that can be used here. One is adding new value by either augmenting the product with more features and/or services or reducing costs. Another approach is repositioning, including brand refocusing and breakaway positioning. Still another is extending the base through new users, new uses, increased use, and line extensions (perhaps moving from sustaining growth to progressive growth). Think about what customers are trying to accomplish when they use your product or service. What job are they "hiring" the product for?

Add New Value

Value is the ratio of benefits to costs. The more benefits a solution provides (in terms of superior features, convenience, simplicity, trust, etc.) relative to costs (price, aggravation, inconsistency, etc.), the higher the perceived value is. Tide, for example, has continued to dominate the detergent market 65 years after its introduction through continuous incremental innovation. It has introduced an average of one brand-related innovation each year since it was launched. Some of the major brand extensions designed to provide new value included Liquid Tide, Tide with Bleach, and Tide Ultra Concentrated.

One approach to thinking through new value is to use a series of "what if" questions related to your products, services, revenue streams, and business models (similar to the questions in Figure 2–3). What would happen if some features were magnified? For example, magnifying the screen on a television contributed to a new market for home theater. Increasing the size of sandwiches shifted the focus from one person to a group. Minimization also can

FIGURE 2-3 ➤ "What if?" decision tree

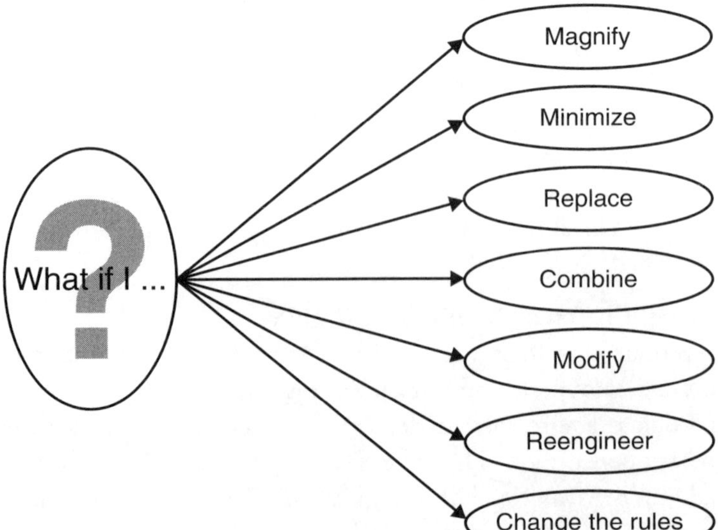

generate new ideas. Reducing the size of television screens created sports TVs. Twitter, as a form of microblogging, also fits this idea of miniaturization. Every market has some segments that are more demanding and some that are less demanding. If specific features are of relatively low importance or value to some customers, can you minimize or eliminate them to provide more value?

What if a new feature replaced an old one? Sony, for example, created the Walkman by replacing speakers with a headset. Cell phones have apps that allow them to act as credit cards. William McDonough's *Cradle to Cradle* was manufactured with pages made of synthetic material rather than paper.

Can two existing products be combined to provide one with more value to the customer? The minivan combined the advantages of a station wagon with those of a van. The tent cot, available through sporting goods retailers, combines a portable cot with the coverage of a tent. Sometimes business units can bundle their products to create more value than would be gotten by selling either one separately to the customer.

Can certain elements be modified? Can standard features become options? Can optional features become standard? This could include both product features and ancillary services. Modifications to sales approaches, contract terms, or technical support can change the product's solution and value.

Think about opportunities for reengineering. Can the development process be reengineered to reduce the overall cost of producing the product or service? Many training programs have been modified with e-learning modules to reduce time and travel costs. Companies such as GE have begun reverse innovation, in which products are created in a developing country for use in that country and for selected applications in developed countries.

Finally, some companies have begun to change the rules in their industry. Software as a service is shifting the purchase of software applications (via downloads and CDs for a particular computer) to purchase of the use of the software (with the actual program housed on the supplier's server).

Reposition

Creating a new competitive posture (in other words, repositioning) can give new life to some customer offerings. As was mentioned earlier, Procter & Gamble has pursued incremental innovations actively to keep Tide fresh, but it also has found it necessary to reposition the brand. In the mid–2000s the brand team began to realize that a series of long-term changes in society had resulted in a decline in Tide's household penetration and required rethinking the brand positioning. Although women still did the bulk of the family laundry, their lives and perspectives had changed. Therefore, the team conducted several ethnographic and market research projects to understand trends and behavioral shifts. They discovered that consumers felt Tide was out of touch with their lives and was "arrogant." On the basis of those insights, they repositioned the brand to connect with their understanding of women's multiple roles. The repositioning reversed the decline and resulted in an increase in market share.

Extend the Base

Another renewal tactic is to boost sales volume by increasing the number of users and/or the usage rate per user. The number of users can be increased by winning competitors' customers, entering new market segments, and/or converting nonusers into users. Volume also can be increased by finding new applications for the product or encouraging more frequent use.

Sometimes the usage and users can be significantly different from the status quo, especially in the latter phases of the product life cycle. Superior Clay Corporation, for example, was a successful manufacturer of clay sewer pipes. As plastic pipes made most applications of clay sewer pipe obsolete, the company found it necessary to reinvent its product line. By reevaluating its competencies, it discovered it could transfer its clay-making capabilities to new products such as fireplace flue liners and decorative chimney pots. By extending its customer base to the new applications, Superior Clay became even more successful than it had been initially.

Relaunch

Relaunched (or resurrected) products are those which have been ignored or even discontinued but seem to have value in the current environment. This could be due to technology growth, change in the competitive arena, or even a sense of nostalgia. These products may generate revenues through a relaunch campaign. The relaunch of an existing product is a more extreme example of renewal and revitalization strategies, which sometimes can be incremental and subtle. If an unused brand is going to be reborn or if a product's repositioning is extensive, it may be useful to give it the same planning one would do for a new product launch.

Rain Bird, a manufacturer of sprinklers and irrigation systems, found that one of its products, DC–6, was unusually successful at one of its retail accounts. Further research uncovered an underserved market. The company redesigned and renamed the product, changed the messaging, and relaunched it at a small fraction of the normal cost associated with new product development.

Rationalization Decisions and Retirement Strategies

Finally, offerings that are clearly not competitive in the product category or are at the end of their life cycle are candidates for elimination (or retirement).

These products are identified by a noted decline in sales, a lack of ability to achieve goals, or the development of a superior product that redefined functionality. Products in this category can pose unique challenges when a key customer clings to the product despite its unprofitable status to your firm.

Note that there are two things to think about here: a decision-making process followed by strategies. Nearly all product lines could benefit from rationalization, which is the systematic analysis and modification of product lines to align them with long-term goals and changing customer need sets. In fact, most firms would become more profitable if they eliminated weak brands and products, and the resources could be better allocated to various growth initiatives. Too much product variety (high complexity) tends to translate into less efficient utilization of assets.

What criteria should you use to identify candidates for pruning? David Anderson has developed the following typical criteria for the process of review and consolidation:

1. *Sales volume:* List sales volumes in a bar chart format over time, in Pareto order.
2. *Sales revenue:* Similarly plot sales revenue.
3. *Part commonality:* Plot products by percentage of common parts.
4. *Cost of variety:* Determine and plot variety costs as a multiplier of baseline products.
5. *True profitability:* At a minimum, plot profit contributions without artificial allocations.
6. *Polls and surveys:* Get input from various experts.
7. *Factory processing:* Determine compatibility with manufacturing processes.
8. *Functionality:* Find opportunities to consolidate products with similar functionalities.
9. *Customer needs:* Determine impact on customers if eliminated.
10. *Core competencies:* These are based on the firm's clear core competencies.
11. *Clean-sheet-of-paper scenario:* Would you have this product if you were a new competitor?
12. *Future potential:* Does the product offer leverage for the future?

After identifying the weak products, you must make decisions and recommendations about what to do with them. As is discussed in Chapter 5, it's useful to generate several alternatives for dealing with the defined weak product. Should the price be lowered to stimulate sales and empty the warehouse?

Should the price be raised to encourage customers to shift to a substitute product? Should the product be sold or licensed to another company?

Most of the discussion on sustaining growth covered strategy differences, many of which did not require significant business model realignments. That is the essence of growth from the core. Now the focus shifts to transformative growth and disruptive growth.

TRANSFORMATIVE GROWTH

Some of the examples in the last category may have sounded suspiciously like progressively moving from the core market into adjacent markets. Obviously, there is not a solid wall between them. It's a matter of increasingly leveraging your ability to create value beyond your core business. With transformative growth, you tweak, shift, morph, and reframe your business model to focus on an expanded customer base (adjacent markets) with new value propositions. Over time these incremental moves into adjacencies can redefine the core business fundamentally.

As shown in Figure 2-4, transformative growth comes from transitioning into adjacent markets and/or better utilizing or expanding competencies, whether internal or external. Figure 2-4 provides a diagram of initiatives that might flow from transitions in customer focus or value proposition. Customer focus and value are inextricably linked, since the perception of value is defined by the groups (usually customers) that provide the revenue for that value. Can you leverage your assets in different ways to provide more value to existing customers? Can you rethink the way you capture value (e.g., using leasing, subscriptions, and other alternatives to your traditional pricing)? What is the opportunity for growth in new industries or countries?

Sometimes it's possible to use an underexploited capability or asset as an engine for growth. McDonald's historically provided fast-food lunches as its core business, but that left the building underutilized at other times of the day. By broadening its menu to include more breakfast items, the company was able to leverage its fixed assets and appeal to a different set of customers.

Publishers, as was mentioned earlier, are adding digital versions of their printed products. This allows them to continue using some existing editorial competencies while extending product form and function. Many are experimenting with alternative revenue streams from online subscriptions and various fee-after-free download options.

A somewhat contrarian approach could be considered. Rather than adding more features to a product, you can strip it to its baseline state and then decide how you can augment it for specific customers. Dow, for example,

FIGURE 2-4 ➤ Transformative growth

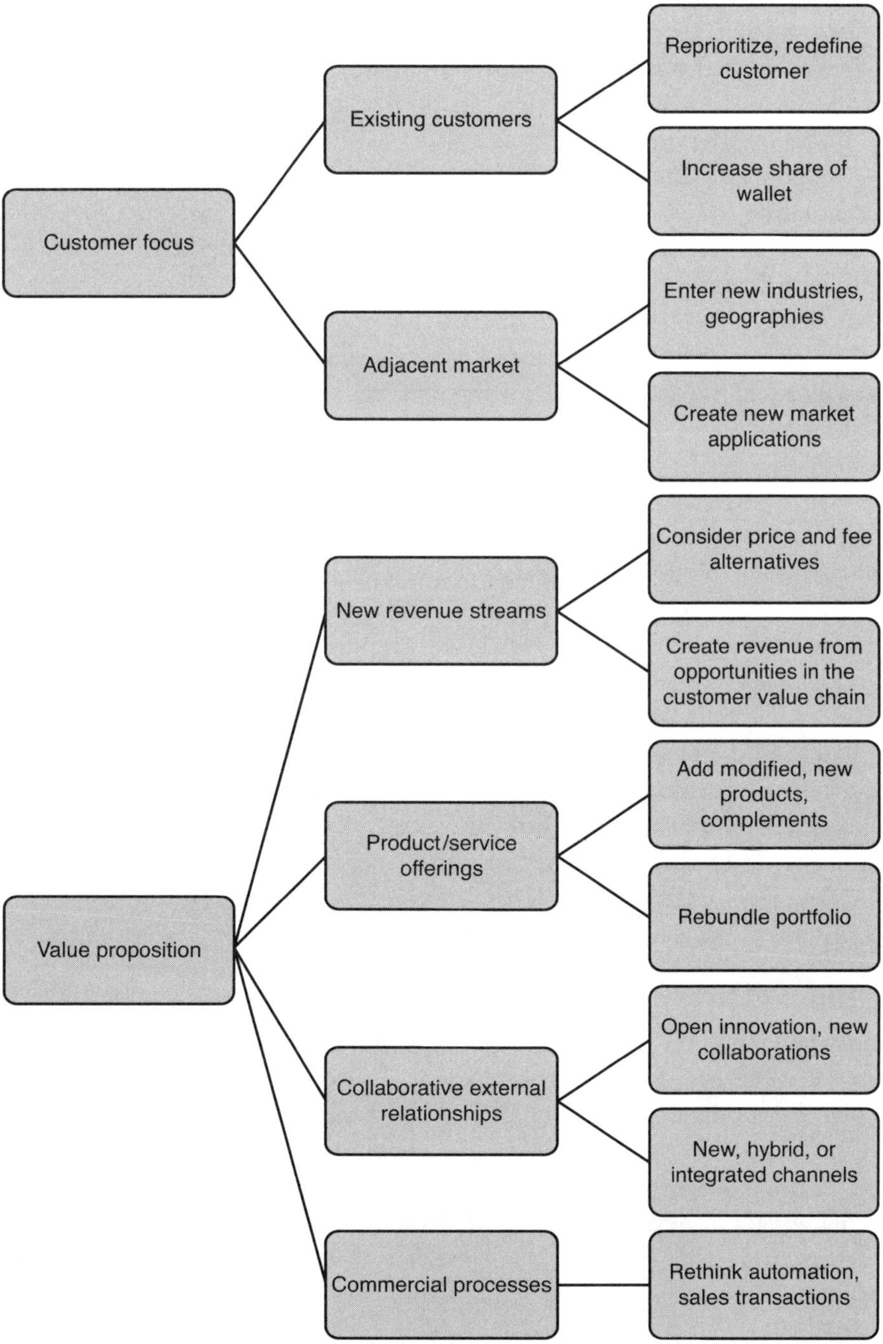

determined that many of its customers wanted to buy silicon in bulk without additional services (known as a naked solution). Thus, in 2002 it created a new brand (Xiameter) and a new business model (using e-commerce) to appeal to that set of customers. Unlike the standard Dow business model of selling the silicon and silicone through the sales force, Xiameter could be purchase online without technical support from sales; however, support was available on a fee-for-service basis.

Technology has transformed the way customers shop in many industries, from online purchases of items to the use of cell phones in stores. Therefore, brick-and-mortar retailers are attempting to embed mobile-device technologies into their business models. Home Depot, for example, has a mobile app that allows consumers to order merchandise on their iPhones. Retailers in other countries have enabled the use of mobile devices as credit cards and/or for downloading relevant information about particular merchandise. An important unknown piece of information here is how customers will shop in the future, and so business models will have to be able to adapt to several plausible futures.

Another transformative growth strategy is moving progressively into global markets. Global strategy often means embedding both domestic and international standards into products and services at the point of design, not as afterthoughts. This implies meeting world standards while simultaneously acknowledging national differences and local norms. This approach has the obvious advantage of taking into consideration the needs of major markets right at the start rather than having to retrofit a product developed for one national market.

It's important to start by identifying globally strategic markets and then analyzing the needs of those markets. By searching for commonalities (as well as differences), managers necessarily think in terms of platform design for global products. Try to design the largest possible standardized core while allowing for necessary customization at the same time. The main goal of the product-development process is not to develop a standard product or product line but to build adaptability into products and product lines to achieve worldwide appeal.

The idea of a fully standardized global product that is identical all over the world is a near myth. Some of the benefits of global products (or services), however, can be achieved by standardizing the core product or large parts of it while customizing peripheral or other parts of the product.

Regardless of the attempt to standardize products or product lines globally, various levels of adaptation are required. Some products require only different language documentation. For example, in the 1990s when Minolta cameras were shipped from Japan to New Wave Enterprise, a distribution center at the port of Antwerp in Belgium, they were shipped without support materials. Language-specific documentation (e.g., French, Dutch, and

German) was added when the products were shipped by land to other destinations in Europe.

Product strategy can vary across a continuum from (1) a nearly universal product (with just labeling and language differences), to (2) a modified product in which the core is standard with adaptations (such as voltage and color) made to reflect local differences, to (3) country-specific products in which the physical product is tailored to the needs of each country or group of countries. The approach to take depends on the variability of market demands.

Research on global brands also suggests new insights into how consumers perceive them. Holt, Quelch, and Taylor conducted a 2004 study based on surveys of 1,800 people in 12 nations. The results, which were published in *Harvard Business Review*, revealed that consumers all over the world associated global brands with three dimensions. The first dimension is a symbol of quality. Consumers believed that since transnational companies must compete more fiercely to develop new products and technologies faster than the competition, they offer more quality and better guarantees. It's interesting to note that this attitude was not directly related to the country of origin but simply to being a global brand. The second dimension is a sense of a global culture. Consumers looked to the brands as "symbols of cultural ideals." The third dimension was social responsibility. The respondents in the study expected global firms to address social problems, to act as "stewards of public health, worker rights, and the environment."

In other situations products could have their life cycles extended by looking for the best fit between market needs and product capabilities. For example, the current U.S. technology for anesthesia ventilators allows plus or minus a few milliliters of oxygen accuracy. However, many hospital operating rooms in developing countries are satisfied with plus or minus 100 milliliters of accuracy, with a commensurately lower price. A major supplier of anesthesia equipment found it could prolong the life of its "unsophisticated" ventilators by offering them in those markets at a much lower price than that of the state-of-the-art equipment.

This approach can apply to consumer products as well. Take basic flour as an example. Several years ago, India was consuming about 69 million tons of wheat a year (compared with 26 million tons in the United States), yet almost no whole-wheat flour was sold prepackaged. Selling packaged flour in India was almost revolutionary, since most Indian housewives still bought raw wheat in bulk, cleaned it by hand, and on a weekly basis carried some to a neighborhood mill, or *chakki*, where it was ground between two stones. Pillsbury found it could increase the sales of basic prepackaged flour (a mature product in the United States) by appealing to this market and modified the Pillsbury Doughboy to pitch this old product as something new in India.

Glocalization refers to the adage "think globally, act locally." Whether you are selling a unique product in every country or a standard product throughout the world, the most effective international strategies still require understanding the local customers. There also may be a set of local competitors that is different from those at the global level.

Start with the basics. How homogeneous is the country or region of interest? Segment the market into reasonable clusters of potential customers and decide which one or ones you will target actively. This could form the foundation of a product line strategy for that area. Do the characteristics of any of the segments transcend national borders? Sometimes younger generations are more like their global counterparts than they are like other generations within their own country. If that is the case, they may be more open to a standardized global product.

In dealing with developing countries, price may be a bigger issue than multinationals have accepted historically. This can pose a challenge, especially for managers who are expected to sell a relatively high-priced product that was designed in a more developed country and can't hit the local price point expectations. These managers have to (1) seek out thought leaders and innovators who may be willing to buy the product at the higher price point, (2) persuade corporate managers of the need to close the cost gap with local companies to come closer to the competitive price point, and/or (3) use reverse innovation. Reverse innovation refers to developing lower-cost products in and for developing countries and then finding applications for them in developed countries.

Managers will need to determine the best method of distribution into the new market. Most firms initially enter other countries through either indirect or direct exporting. *Indirect* exporting refers to selling through a domestically based intermediary (e.g., agent or distributor). The major benefits of this approach lie in the ease of administration. Even companies with little or no experience in exporting can rely on the expertise of the channel partner without developing substantial multinational cultural skills. With *direct* exporting, the manufacturer deals directly with foreign intermediaries in the distribution of its products. Although this approach requires a greater degree of cultural expertise, it also provides the firm with more market knowledge and potentially greater control.

In a *Harvard Business Review* article, David Arnold states that the selection of international business partners is especially critical because of the distances and cultures of the buying parties. He elaborates on seven key points in selecting and working with international distributors and trading partners:

1. "Select distributors. Don't let them select you." The key point is to choose markets first and then select distributors and agents.

2. "Look for distributors capable of developing markets, rather than those with a few obvious customer contacts." Select partners who are willing to invest and grow the markets.
3. "Treat the local distributors as long-term partners, not temporary market-entry vehicles." Create an atmosphere that fosters appropriate goals, such as customer acquisition and retention, new product sales, collaborative inventory management, and replenishment.
4. "Support market entry by committing money, managers, and proven marketing ideas." Invest in product modifications to meet the needs of local markets and personnel support.
5. "From the start, maintain control over marketing strategy." Managers should visit distributors and channel members to learn about the local market.
6. "Make sure distributors provide you with detailed market and financial performance data." Develop relationships and contracts that share detailed market data and financial performance.
7. "Build links among national distributors at the earliest opportunity." Just as in the home country, distributors meet and build relationships to share experiences. Help all parties improve their success in marketing efforts.

DISRUPTIVE GROWTH

More substantial change is implied in this third category. Disruptive growth refers to creating something new to the world or at a minimum establishing a dramatically different business model for your organization. They can be "bet-the-farm" propositions if they are stand-alone rather than part of a portfolio. That's why for existing companies they are likely to be part of a broader look at business model renewal.

Procter & Gamble's FutureWorks is a growth effort focused on enabling different business models, some transformative and others disruptive. The firm's more disruptive models involve franchised service-based businesses that leverage the brand strength of existing products. Teams explored how to disrupt the dry-cleaning market, for example, while capitalizing and expanding on P&G's knowledge of consumers' laundry-cleaning perceptions and experiences. According to the P&G FutureWorks website in June 2011, the company opened three Tide Dry Cleaners stores in 2008 and is now pursuing franchisees. Similarly, it has tested and is now seeking franchisees for its Mr. Clean Car Wash businesses. Both initiatives moved into new customer markets (for P&G) while building on existing brand strength and consumer knowledge. The new business model also required collaborating with external partners to develop new revenue streams. By hiring Agile Pursuits Franchising, P&G gained franchising knowledge that it would have taken years to develop internally.

Another example of disruptive growth comes from the automotive industry. With increasing interest in renewable energy and the growing market for electric vehicles, many battery manufacturers (such as A123 Systems, Exide, and Johnson Controls) are racing to perfect lithium-ion batteries. But some companies are looking at the potential disruptive growth opportunities inherent in the ecosystem of the electric car industry. In addition to new products, there will be a need for servicing, replacement, and recycling of these products as well as operational recharging to extend the range of driving. Interstate Batteries and Better Place have the potential to establish those disruptive business models.

Interstate Batteries began selling batteries 60 years ago and is America's largest distributor of lead acid batteries, including the types that go into electric cars. It manages private-label replacement batteries for the world's largest automakers. But it is also in the process of opening dozens (and potentially hundreds) of stores for distribution and recycling. CEO Carlos Sepulveda wants to stake a claim as the "RadioShack of renewables."

Better Place, a start-up, is working to build stations for swapping and recharging batteries, analogous to gas stations for traditional cars. One of the significant drawbacks of electric vehicles (EVs) is the time it takes to recharge batteries. When done with a normal standard outlet (110 volts)—referred to as Level 1 charging—it can take longer than overnight. Even with Level 2 (the voltage required for a stove), it would take about six hours. Level 3 is the fastest, but existing batteries are not ready for this type of charging. Another drawback is the shorter driving range of most EVs on a battery pack. That's why battery swapping was conceived as a potential solution.

In his **Dateline interview**, Israeli entrepreneur Shai Agassi shared his vision

http://www.youtube.com/watch?v=ReMZzaj6gdo&feature=player_embedded#!

for transforming the automotive industry from gas to electric vehicles. One of his metaphors to win over skeptics was a comparison to the music industry. He mentioned that the Sony Walkman was the number one music player in 2001. If in 2001 someone had predicted that within 10 years that product would be gone (and replaced by a product from a company outside the industry), most people would not have believed it. Yet it happened.

NEXT STEPS

As you think about your business model growth portfolio, consider the percentage of time and resources you are willing to commit to sustaining, transformative, and disruptive growth. Select specific initiatives for each potential growth strategy and plan an appropriate course of action. Be sure to have the commitment of the most appropriate team of players in the company, a group that has the credibility and authority to make things happen. Teach the team members the mindsets and mental models (such as foresight) that foster creative thinking across all categories of growth. Create a process manual that has step-by-step guides to help jump-start progress, especially for transformative and disruptive projects. Create a culture of rapidly prototyping and testing new business models. Stage the investments to allow flexibility before all operational plans are carved in stone. Finally, encourage cross-pollination of ideas throughout the organization as well as from ideas external to the firm.

BOB ARZBAECHER

SUSTAINABLE GROWTH WITHOUT RADICAL CHANGE

Robert (Bob) C. Arzbaecher has been president and chief executive officer of Actuant Corporation (formerly Applied Power Inc.) since August 9, 2000. Previous positions with the firm included senior vice president and chief financial officer; vice president and chief financial officer; vice president, finance; and corporate controller. Before joining Applied Power, Arzbaecher served as chief financial officer for Grabill Aerospace Industries Ltd. and held various financial positions with Farley Industries and Grant Thornton, a public accounting firm. He has been chairman of Actuant since 2001 and its director since August 9, 2000.

Robert C. Arzbaecher
President and Chief Executive Officer
Actuant Corporation

Bob, you've been a long-term employee and you are the current chairman and CEO of Actuant. So before we get to the questions about the company, can you talk a bit about your career path at Actuant and how you progressed to your current leadership position?

My career with Actuant and its predecessor company, Applied Power, began in 1992 as corporate controller. I moved around various financial leadership positions within the company until 1995, when I became chief financial officer. From 1996 to 1999 Applied Power conducted an acquisition roll-up strategy in the electronic enclosures space, acquiring four sizable businesses with sales totaling $1.1 billion.

At that time, Applied Power made the strategic decision to split the company into two separately traded public companies. APW represented the electronic enclosures business, and Actuant accounted for the industrial businesses. I was made CEO of Actuant in early 2000, and the spin-off of APW was completed in August 2000. At the time, our sales were $400 million and our market capitalization was under $200 million.

You've been pretty up front about the need to switch from defense to offense to take advantage of new opportunities. What are some of the factors that caused you to move in this direction, and what are some of the steps you've taken to actually make the shift?

The move from defense to offense has been evolutionary for Actuant, starting almost immediately after the spin-off in 2000. At that time, we had our first successes with kanban and kaizen events at our Enerpac business unit, and this was the start of a long and never-ending journey of continuous improvement across the entire Actuant organization.

In December 2004, we completed a secondary equity offering which allowed us to pay down our debt to a reasonable level. We began to think about our second growth strategy: growth through acquisitions. Since that date we have completed 24 transactions deploying approximately $1.3 billion of capital.

Finally, in May 2010 we launched our third offensive strategy: our growth and innovation initiative. This is a formalized internal growth process where we look to:

- Drive new product development to sell into existing markets
- Take existing products into new end markets
- Aggressively expand our emerging-market presence

One of the strategic focus areas you mentioned is continuous improvement. What are some of your efforts to advance the culture of continuous improvement across Actuant?

Continuous improvement is a hallmark of our LEAD (Lean Enterprise Across Disciplines) program. We look to improve sales, profitability, and asset efficiency. Culturally, we hire people who understand lean principles; we utilize a small group of people in the LEAD office to help the operating companies with their continuous improvement program, and we offer a great deal of training in the foundations of lean to employees worldwide. Finally, all of our variable compensation is tied to improvement, both the income statement and balance sheet efficiency. Nonstop communication, along with using LEAD every day in our business lives, is essential if you're going to embed it in the culture.

Can you talk more about your growth and innovation focus? How are you balancing organic and inorganic growth in this initiative, and how does this fit into your business model?

We've had inorganic growth through acquisition as a key part of our strategy for many years, so we really haven't had to change our approach to this. What we have done is reemphasize organic growth by putting in place processes, metrics, and resources—approximately 50 people to date—to build our growth and innovation process. We don't find it an either-or trade-off; we expect both.

What we like about the Michael Treacy growth and innovation model which we've adopted is that it treats growth as a *process*, similar to our current cost-focused LEAD initiatives. This is making it easier for our "process"-oriented culture to adopt.

If you were to give advice to executives rethinking their business models, what are the top three or four things you would tell them?

1. Look for incremental versus transformation change. Execute on enough incremental changes over a few years and you will look back and decide you created transformational change.
2. Focus on cash flow and ROIC (return on invested capital). Other metrics should support this overarching focus.
3. Focus on what your customers are saying. Do you have processes to capture accurate voice of customer (VOC)?
4. Emphasize emerging markets. Where are your best opportunities, and what might emerging markets do to your existing business model?

REFERENCES

Anderson, David M., and B. Joseph Pine II, *Agile Product Development for Mass Customization*, Times Mirror, 1997.

Andersson, Roy, Henrik Eriksson, and Hakan Torstensson, "Similarities and Differences between TQM, Six Sigma and Lean," *TQM Magazine,* 2006, vol. 18, issue 3, p. 282.

Andrews, Kenneth R., *The Concept of Corporate Strategy*, Irwin, 1971.

Arnold, David, "Seven Rules of International Business," *Harvard Business Review,* November–December 2000, pp. 131–137.

Barwise, Patrick, Sean Meehan, and Emma MacDonald, "Relentless Tide: An Unstoppable Megabrand," *Business Strategy Review*, Summer 2011, pp. 59–63.

Bettencourt, Lance A., and Scott L. Bettencourt, "Innovating on the Cheap," *Harvard Business Review*, June 2011, pp. 88–94.

Brown, Bruce, and Scott D. Anthony, "How P&G Tripled its Innovation Success Rate," *Harvard Business Review*, June 2011, pp. 65–72.

Christensen, Clayton M., *The Innovator's Dilemma: The Revolutionary Book That Will Change the Way You Do Business*, Harper Paperbacks, 2003.

Christensen, Clayton, M., and Michael E. Raynor, *The Innovator's Solution: Creating and Sustaining Successful Growth*, Harvard Business Press, 2003.

Collins, Jim, and Jerry I. Porras, *Built to Last: Successful Habits of Visionary Companies*, HarperBusiness, 2004.

Collis, David, and Cynthia Montgomery, "Competing on Resources," *Harvard Business Review*, July–August 1995, pp. 118–129.

Davis, Ian, "How to Escape the Short-Term Trap," *McKinsey Quarterly* (online), April 2005.

Day, George S., *Market Driven Strategy: Processes for Creating Value*, Free Press, 1999.

Dinesh, David, and Elaine Palmer, "Management by Objectives and the Balanced Scorecard: Will Rome Fall Again?" *Management Decision*, London, 1998, vol. 36, issue 6, p. 363.

Friday-Stroud, Shawnta S., and J. Scott Sutterfield, "A Conceptual Framework for Integrating Six Sigma and Strategic Management Methodologies to Quantify Decision Making," *TQM Magazine*, 2007, vol. 19, issue 6, p. 561.

Gladwell, Malcolm, *The Tipping Point: How Little Things Can Make a Big Difference*, Back Bay Books, 2002.

Gorchels, Linda, *The Product Manager's Handbook*, 4th ed., McGraw-Hill, 2011.

Gunther, Marc, "3M's Innovation Revival," *CNNMoney.com*, September 24, 2010.

Holt, Douglas B., John A. Quelch, and Earl L. Taylor, "How Global Brands Compete," *Harvard Business Review*, September 2004, pp. 68–75.

Kim, W. Chan, and Renee Mauborgne, *Blue Ocean Strategy: How to Create Uncontested Market Space and Make Competition Irrelevant*, Harvard Business Press, 2005.

Lindsay, Greg, "The RadioShack of Renewables," *Fast Company*, December 2010–January 2011, p. 53.

McGrath, Rita Gunther, and Ian C. MacMillan, *MarketBusters: 40 Strategic Moves That Drive Exceptional Business Growth*, Harvard Business Press, 2005.

Peters, Thomas J., and Robert H. Waterman, *In Search of Excellence: Lessons from America's Best-Run Companies*, Harper Paperbacks, 1982 (republished in 2004).

Phillips, Anne, "Charging Up," *Summit*, May 2011, pp. 14–18.

Pillet, Maurice, and Jean-Luc Maire, "How to Sustain Improvement at High Level: Application in the Field of Statistical Process Control," *TQM Journal*, 2008, vol. 20, issue 6, p. 570.

Porter, Michael E., "The Five Competitive Forces That Shape Strategy," *Harvard Business Review*, January 2008, p. 78. First published by *Harvard Business Review* as the 1979 article "How Competitive Forces Shape Strategy"; also can be found in Porter, *Competitive Strategy: Techniques for Analyzing Industries and Competitors*, Free Press, 1998.

Prahalad, C. K. and Gary Hamel, "The Core Competence of the Corporation," *Harvard Business Review*, May–June 1990, p. 79.

Reingold, Jennifer, and Ryan Underwood, "Was *Built to Last* Built to Last?" *Fast Company*, December 19, 2007, pp. 102–108.

Salmon, Felix, "Wall Street's Dead End," *New York Times*, February 13, 2011, p. A27.

Treacy, Michael, and Fred Wiersema, *The Discipline of Market Leaders: Choose Your Customers, Narrow Your Focus, Dominate Your Market*, Basic Books, 1997.

Zook, Chris, and James Allen, *Profit from the Core: A Return to Growth in Turbulent Times*, Harvard Business Press, 2010.

PART 2

Mental Models and Insights

This section describes some of the mental models (or mindsets) necessary to escape short-term myopia. Chapter 3 explores the topic of foresight, or the study of the future. It highlights the importance of a systems perspective and critical thinking skills and helps provide a context, especially for transformative growth and disruptive growth. Chapter 4 examines innovation from both a new product perspective and an organizational perspective. It considers decisions about innovating to improve customer value as well as to improve business model alignment. Chapter 5 rounds out this section with a look at the biases that influence the decision-making process.

CHAPTER 3

Foresight: Betting on Turbulence

A few years ago I attended a certificate program in strategic foresight at the University of Houston. The class consisted of a cadre of individuals from the military, national security, think tanks, corporations, and higher education. This was a highly diverse group whose members shared approaches to anticipating and preparing for the future. It challenged me to think about foresight as a mental model, an expansive collection of thought processes that goes beyond traditional economic, statistical, and business forecasting to include judgment and qualitative inputs. Rather than simply extrapolating current and past trends, foresight is the act of looking forward in an effort to prepare for the future, and it's becoming an increasingly important part of business acumen.

Business acumen requires both science and art, with a need to balance day-to-day operational and fiscal demands with longer-term expectations for growth. It becomes particularly challenging when the demand for short-term results crowds out creative thinking. In fact, many of the tools and techniques of traditional business planning are directly contrary to what is needed for the strategic side of business acumen. Leaders must avoid simply managing a budget when they should be managing their organizations for the future. That is when the mental models of foresight become relevant.

EVERY BUSINESS DECISION IS A BET ON THE FUTURE

Foresight methods, many of which were developed by the RAND Corporation, have been used for years, typically for global and military planning. Unlike forecasting, in which individuals attempt to predict the future, foresight methods recognize that the vast number of interrelated variables makes it impossible to predict the future with any precision. There is an old Arab proverb, "He who predicts the future lies even if he tells the truth." Instead of seeking predictability, leaders use foresight to prepare themselves and their organizations for different contingencies. This helps them steer a course between the false certainty of a precise forecast and the chaos of unexamined circumstances. It requires a possibilities mindset rather than an evidence-based mindset. Many futurists, such as **Steve Tighe**, consider strategic foresight

http://www.youtube.com/watch?v=G_oEtVEoVhc

to be the next major business frontier.

Foresight is defined on Dictionary.com as "care or provision for the future." The Free Dictionary defines it as the "perception of the significance and nature of events before they have occurred." According to Wikipedia, corporate foresight is the ability to detect and interpret change early in order to formulate effective responses; it "is used to support strategic management, identify new business fields, and increase the innovation capacity of a firm." Most foresight practitioners recognize that although the future is unpredictable, it is not predetermined. We can influence it through the actions we take. Following is an excerpt from past promotional literature of the World Future Society that restates this point:

> *If we could predict the future with certainty, it would mean that the future could not be changed. . . . Yet this is the main purpose of studying the future: to look at what may happen if present trends continue, decide if this is what is desirable, and if it's not, work to change it. . . . The ability to see and create the future is the essence of leadership.*

Note the last sentence: "The ability to see and create the future is the essence of leadership." Organizational leaders are continually challenged to develop business models and strategies that enable their organizations to take advantage of future opportunities and minimize possible threats. They must go beyond conventional wisdom; avoid single, simple solutions; and focus on perspective rather than precision. As Peter Bishop, associate professor at the University of Houston and founding member of the Association of Professional Futurists, mentions in his end-of-chapter interview, foresight,

FIGURE 3-1 ➤ Projecting into the future

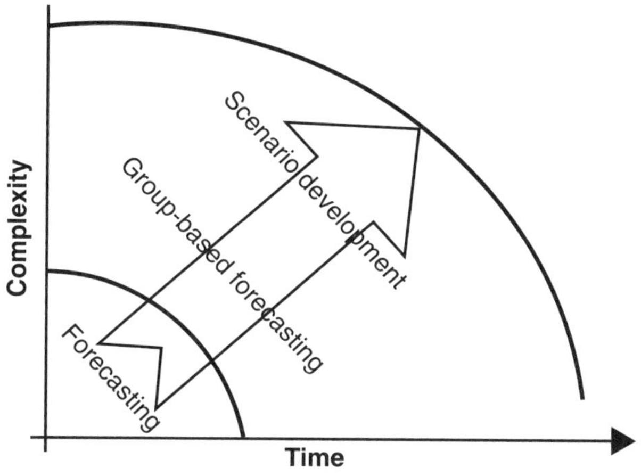

compared with other types of planning, tends to be "more long-term, more visionary, and more transformational, ... [placing a] greater emphasis on broad participation."

Let's dig a bit more deeply into the difference between fore*casting* and fore*sight*. Forecasting is a necessary component of short-term and annual operating plans. Companies need to commit specific resources and assets to generate positive cash flows. Therefore, a variety of forecasts (from sales force estimates, to internal trend projections, to customer research) are compiled and then reconciled to allow the establishment of budgets. Forecasting and mathematical modeling are necessary for a detailed understanding of specific issues over shorter time frames (see Figure 3-1). The more complex and the farther into the future the projections are intended to be, the more usefulness shifts from forecasting to group-based forecasting to scenario development.

Foresight is less predictive. Its purpose is not to generate numbers to drive budgets immediately but to generate perspective to open minds. The objective is to stimulate, inform, and prepare people for a variety of future possibilities. The techniques are most valuable if they allow decision makers to understand the potential strategic implications of the alternative futures more fully.

Foresight techniques include several methods that are applied in an attempt to examine a range of plausible futures. Scenario development is perhaps the most commonly used technique. However, companies have experimented with group-based forecasting and ideation using options such as Delphi, prediction markets, integrated roadmapping, and social media options. All of these techniques are described in this chapter.

SCENARIO DEVELOPMENT

Scenario development is a systematic way of envisioning alternative futures by telling stories about how the future might unfold for your particular organization. It is a more dynamic strategic planning process that "forces" executives to look across a range of options and manage toward the one they think most likely to prevail. Rather than approaching it from a mindset of forecasting, it should build a sense of flexibility to encourage adaptation in the present. The goal is to increase an organization's readiness for a range of possibilities.

Because the past may not be a good predictor of the future, scenario planning encourages organizations to consider how demographics, globalization, technology, and other changes will shape the future. By doing this, decision makers can both mitigate risk and decrease the likelihood of being unprepared for discontinuities. They can challenge their own entrenched mental models and assumptions and anticipate a broader set of future possibilities. That's why scenario planning has been used by companies as diverse as Disney, Royal Dutch Shell, General Electric, and UPS, along with governmental agencies in many countries.

Global scenarios have been part of Shell's corporate culture for decades. In 2005, the company published for the public for the first time its Shell Global Scenarios to 2025. Shell director Jeremy Bentham talked about the value of this approach in his **YouTube video** on the topic. In

http://www.youtube.com/watch?v=tzlnB_MszyM

preparing the treatise, a team of internal and external experts examined the legal environments, the international markets, the geopolitics, and the complex interplay among them to arrive at three plausible futures for the industry's global business environment. The three scenarios arrived at were (1) Low Trust Globalization, (2) Open Doors, and (3) Flags.

The Low Trust Globalization scenario defines a "prove it to me" world in which corporate interactions place heavy emphasis on regulation and litigation. The Open Doors scenario assumes a world in which government acts in the background and organizations voluntarily follow best-practice codes. The Flags scenario is more nationally dogmatic, with businesses maintaining strong national identities. These three scenarios are stories about what the global oil industry could look like in 2025. They are not predictive but instead are intended to help leaders be open to trends and options before developing go-forward plans. Looking 20 years into the future, all three of these scenarios are plausible. The true value of thinking through the three scenarios lies in avoiding the myopia of assuming that one long-term forecasted direction is sufficient for crafting strategies and business models.

Process of Scenario Development

Companies typically follow several steps as they build scenarios: (1) define the scenario development team, (2) identify drivers of change, (3) create scenarios, (4) determine how to be successful in each of the scenarios, (5) seek common or agile components and establish strategic direction. These steps are depicted graphically in Figure 3-2.

Define the Scenario Development Team

Comprehensive scenarios rarely are developed by one person. It is too easy to overlook key factors that could have a significant impact on the future. Try to get involvement from people with diverse perspectives, not just people from different functions. Shell's scenario team for its Global Scenarios to 2025 included both internal and external experts. Some of the internal authorities were the group's chief economist, the head of its energy team, the chief political

FIGURE 3-2 ➤ Process of Scenario Development

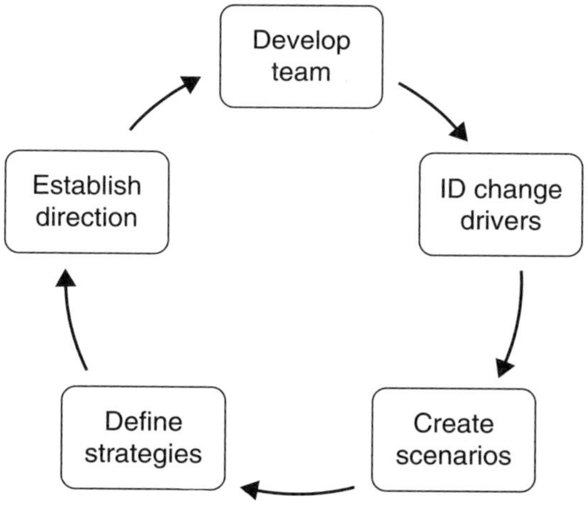

analyst, and members of group strategy and planning, among others. They solicited input from numerous internal colleagues, some of whom oversaw or took part in scenario exercises. They also received insight from a multitude of experts from centers of excellence in academia, consulting, and think tanks.

Although this is more elaborate than may be viable or even appropriate for other organizations, it highlights the need to think broadly. Beyond key functional managers, get a local futurist, economist, behavioral scientist, physician, statistician, technology analyst, or another credible adviser to participate as part of your scenario development team. Solicit input from your CPA, sister business units, the board of directors, supply chain partners, or others who may have a vested interest and are able to contribute ideas different from your own. Decide who will be sustaining members of the scenario development team and who will be occasional contributors.

Identify Drivers of Change

Once the team is in place, the next step is to define the external variables (drivers) assumed to have the greatest likelihood of causing or contributing to change in the future. (Ideally, you have brought together people who are knowledgeable about the identified drivers of change, but if you have not, you can still add them to the team.) Sometimes it's useful to start with typical categories such as the TIME (technology, industry, market, and event) categories discussed in Chapter 1.

Either as a premeeting homework assignment or as a brainstorming exercise during the meeting, the team should identify technological innovations, industry shifts, market/societal/ demographic forces, or political/economic/environmental/regulatory events that have the potential to change your organization's future within the time cycle of your planning process. Determine which drivers are relatively knowable (e.g., you can predict the aging of the population) and which could be dramatically different in the future. Focus most on drivers that differentiate alternative futures from one another.

Next the team should evaluate the drivers of change in terms of importance to your organization and the probability and impact of their occurring within the allotted time frame. Drivers that would have a significant impact on your strategy or business model *and* have at least a moderate probability of occurring should rise to the top. A common evaluation process is to have each team member "vote" with stickers or Post-it notes.

It's important to remember that both the identification of the potential change drivers and the evaluation of their significance depend on individual assumptions. Encourage the team members to acknowledge and "stress-test" their assumptions. What would it take for the assumption to be invalidated?

When individuals prepare for the future, the vast majority of them don't take the time to explore the fit of the past and present with the future. Our projections are based on theories (what we *think* we know) and assumptions (what we *believe* we know). If these are incorrect or go unexamined, we may move in the wrong direction into the future.

Create Scenarios

Once the key drivers are agreed on, hypothesize what the extremes of that particular variable could be. For example, assume that a key change driver for an employer-benefits-based health insurer is the existence of a retail insurance exchange. The extremes could be a fully functioning exchange in which individuals can obtain health insurance directly and individually on one end and the elimination of that possibility at the other end. Do the same thing for the remaining drivers.

Now it's time to create stories about the future. How do the drivers relate to one another? Is a high extreme on one related to a low extreme on another? What combinations of levels of each driver are reasonable and plausible scenarios? Try to craft the information into three to five scenarios, each with a description of a paragraph or so. Then title each scenario. In 2006 Sai Ma and Michael Seid published a disease management scenario planning case in *Health Care Management Review*. In that article they provided a snapshot of eight plausible alternative healthcare futures for 2020, which they named (1) Health Care Utopia, (2) Provider Squeeze, (3) Free Market Bliss, (4) More Freedom, Less Choice, (5) Big Brother, (6) The Golden Rule, (7) Pharma Techno Oligarchy, and (8) Descent to Chaos. Here is their description of the scenario titled Pharma Techno Oligarchy:

> *Multinational corporations that control pharmaceutical and health information technology have grown exponentially; much of the data used by these corporations is proprietary; patents continue to be rigorously enforced. Direct-to-consumer advertising is the primary means by which most people understand their health care; consumers have trouble understanding the overwhelming, often contradictory, information on the Internet and lack the ability to determine quality at the provider level. In this world, payers are very diffuse and each has little purchasing power. On the other hand, pharma-techno companies are so powerful that they actually drive and decide the demand side through advertising, lobbying, and supplying what they want to supply. As a result, cost of treatments (drugs, surgeries) could be very high due to the lack of negotiation power and "wholesale" price. Quality of care might get worse.*

Scenarios are written as plausible futures, not as probable futures. They are intended to invoke the imagination rather than provide a set of statistical tables. Scenarios help "rehearse the future" by forcing managers to think about decisions required in diverse circumstances. If they accomplish those goals, they should reduce the impact of the unintended consequences that often occurs in plans.

There is no right or wrong way to write the scenarios, since none of the scenarios is likely to describe the future accurately. As long as they are deemed plausible by the team and have sufficient diversity to challenge strategy and business model design, they have accomplished their purpose.

Determine How to Be Successful in Each of the Scenarios

This step involves sketching out at a high level successful strategies for each scenario. Determine your customer definition (where you will compete) and your value proposition (how you might win). As you develop each prototypical strategy, try to address the following questions.

For customer definition:

- What will be the balance between customer acquisition and retention?
- Will new-customer acquisition strategies target similar customers (compared with your current customers) or move into adjacent markets (different demographics, industries, countries)?
- Will customer redefinition be required?
- Does the scenario imply the growth of new customer segments (ones that previously did not exist)?

For value proposition:

- What new products, services, or solutions will be necessary for the defined customers? For these offerings, will you be able to thrive and win? How?
- Will new competencies be possible as a result of changes in technology, regulations, industry profiles, or other factors? What assumptions (if any) would have to be realized for this to happen?
- Are new or additional revenue streams (beyond the product and service offerings sold to customers) plausible under the scenario? What are they?

For business model alignment:

- Is there change readiness in the organizational culture for this strategy? If not, what steps would be necessary to go forward?
- What additional resources and competencies would be needed for implementation? What would it take for your organization to move from where it is now to acquire or develop these new competencies?
- Will this strategy and business model be profitable? What are your assumptions?

Try to be painfully realistic about your current capabilities as well as the capabilities required to implement the strategies identified. Determine whether there are significant gaps as well as what investment might be required to close those gaps. Are the gaps greater for some strategies than for others? What would be the risk posed by a particular scenario happening for which you didn't have the necessary competencies?

Seek Common or Agile Components and Establish Strategic Direction

As has been stated several times, an essential value of scenario development is an examination of a broader range of plausible futures than is typically the case with traditional business planning. But at some point, decisions have to be made on the way forward.

Take a look at each strategy and see how well it would fare in the alternative scenarios. If you are fortunate enough to identify a strategy that is sufficiently robust to work under all scenarios, that simplifies the choice. But it is more likely that some strategies are winners in some scenarios and losers in others. There are a few approaches to consider here. You can estimate the chances of each scenario occurring and select a strategy for each scenario. Another approach is to look for common elements of all (or most) strategies and try to create a modified strategy that minimizes the risk of failure regardless of which of the scenarios comes to pass.

Or you might pursue one dominant strategy and commission small-scale tests of alternative strategies to build agility to respond to unanticipated futures. This requires business model flexibility. Leaders must be willing to support pilot projects, along with dynamic course correction and expedient financial modeling. Lean and scalable processes are necessary to deliver a rapid response platform for growth. This may require a willingness to use variable rather than fixed assets to respond to market conditions faster.

An Example: Corporate Energy Futures

Bill Ralston, coauthor of *The Scenario Planning Handbook*, wrote an article describing components of the process as it relates to future energy scenarios for corporations that are heavy consumers of energy. First he defined several drivers of change or uncertainty, including future energy markets, global climate changes, global environmental values and priorities, and world economic growth. Once the four drivers were determined, he considered the extreme end points for each. Future energy markets could continue to be dominated by abundant hydrocarbons, or there could be a significant shift to renewable alternatives. Global climate could change abruptly or incrementally. In regard to global environmental priorities, there could be overall agreement about reducing emissions or there could be a lack of execution of any policies. Finally, world economic growth could continue to expand at a relatively high rate, or there could be wildly erratic and uneven economic performance everywhere.

After examining the extreme end points of these four drivers, Ralston defined two alternative future scenarios: (1) Roller Coaster and (2) Stuck on Carbon. In the story about the first scenario, there will be a shift to renewables, abrupt climate changes, global agreement on environmental priorities, and the continuation of global economic development. In the second scenario, there will be an abundance of hydrocarbons, incremental climate change, global disagreements on environmental priorities, and economic nationalism. These two scenarios were expanded into fairly descriptive stories.

Next Ralston brainstormed strategy ideas for addressing the threats and opportunities inherent in each of the scenarios. For the Roller Coaster scenario, companies would be advised to reduce the amount of carbon energy they used, perhaps by implementing comprehensive energy efficiency measures. Strategy choices for the Stuck on Carbon scenario might emphasize the importance of economic performance to a greater extent than short-term carbon reduction.

In comparing the strategies, managers need to be mindful of the continued trends, risks, and uncertainties going forward. Some of the questions they should consider include the following: Which strategy components are resilient across both scenarios? What is the risk of implementing them? Are there any signposts to monitor that will help determine which way the trends are evolving? What decisions are irreversible? What is the potential impact on the company if we're wrong? Then, based on the answers to these questions, they should identify the practical actions necessary for implementation.

A Few More Tips on Scenario Development

The very activity of effective scenario development efforts should generate deeper insight into the drivers of change, but it takes time and effort and willingness to suspend disbelief. If it is simply a two-hour brainstorming session, it probably will fail. Allow the process to provide a safe haven for contrarian thinking. Don't ignore extreme scenarios. Since most large organizations have a bias toward the status quo, scenario development may provide a gentle reminder that a current business model or strategy may not be the best option for several plausible futures. It allows an organization to challenge the "official" future, trigger imagination, and incorporate diverse perspectives.

Don't allow your firm to become paralyzed by too many options. That can happen if the final step of the process is ignored. A clear vision and future direction need to be established. Although scenario development helps leaders appreciate a range of potential realities in the future, they nevertheless must aim the strategic compass. Although it is unlikely that leaders will communicate broadly via scenarios (since by then they will be focused on one), the very analysis of a broad range of possibilities lessens the risk of them making statements that will be proved wrong if one of the alternative futures begins to emerge.

GROUP-BASED FORECASTING AND IDEATION

Although scenario planning has gained awareness recently, there are other approaches to foresight, all of which rely on multiplicity of inputs. The Delphi method (a process that has been around since the 1950s) and prediction markets (a newer addition to the foresight toolbox) are group-based techniques designed to reach consensus iteratively. Roadmapping is another technique that sometimes is used to reach consensus, but in other situations it is used to generate ideas and a planning process for innovation. Social networking tools are used primarily for ideation and confirmation (and less for consensus).

The Delphi Method

The technique for arriving at consensus about the future through the Delphi method was developed in the 1950s by a research group at the RAND Corporation. It is an organized process of eliciting expert opinions about specific aspects of the future. Application of the Delphi method is most appropriate in industries in which future forecasts require experts with different profiles, heterogeneous participants, and subjective assessments.

It starts by choosing a panel on the basis of the members' expertise on a particular topic. A facilitator surveys the individual panel members about their beliefs and expectations about how the future will unfold. The anonymity of experts is presumed to avoid the bias, peer pressure, and negative group dynamics associated with face-to-face discussions. After the replies are gathered and summarized, the facilitator shares them with the group, providing anonymous insights from diverse perspectives. Panel members respond to another survey, revising their opinions on the basis of the new information. The process continues until consensus is reached.

As with all tools, there are advantages and disadvantages. Among the advantages, this approach provides an opportunity for a relatively large number of experts to participate. The anonymity of the participants allows a focus on ideas rather than individuals, and it provides an opportunity for the participants to reconsider their opinions without ego or influence.

However, it can take a significant amount of time to conduct several rounds. During that time participant enthusiasm can wane, and there can be a temptation to simplify involvement by simply agreeing with the majority opinion. The consensus on a singular future may prevent managers and leaders from considering a full set of options.

Prediction Markets

Prediction markets also involve gathering inputs from a host of individuals. However, unlike Delphi, they attempt to aggregate the "wisdom of crowds" in the belief that large groups of people are more likely than an elite few to foster innovation and anticipate the future. Some experts liken prediction markets to an online variation of Delphi.

Prediction markets are web based applications that work like hypothetical

http://www.youtube.com/watch?v=9_MXvopRqps

stock markets. Expectations about future events are linked to trading prices that can be interpreted as the probability of an event coming true. Let's say, for example, a company wants input from its employees on whether a particular product launch will occur on time. It creates a "contract" that states that the "investor" will get $100 if the launch is on time and nothing if the launch is delayed. If the aggregate investment causes the contract to trade at $70, this is interpreted as an employee-perceived 70 percent probability of an on-time launch.

Best Buy has experimented with prediction markets, but more from a tactical perspective than from a futures-based perspective. Their prediction market is structured as an imaginary online stock-trading game for employees called **Tag Trade**. All employees can trade fake money in response to issues posed by

http://www.youtube.com/watch?v=keVLOPkCpaQ&feature=related

management, such as how many gift cards the retailer would sell in a specific time period or what sales would be for a new service package. The predictions of the market were sometimes more accurate than were the "official forecasts."

Although prediction markets are used frequently to forecast relatively short-term events, some companies have used them as part of organizational alignment behind a chosen strategy. If the approach is used as a tool for top executives to assess change drivers, agree on key assumptions, and propose strategic initiatives, the time it takes for evaluating and aggregating strategic decisions may be shortened.

Numerous companies provide the technology to support enterprise or corporate prediction markets. Crowdcast's website lists Hershey's, Boeing, and Harvard as some of its clients. Consensus Point lists Best Buy, General Electric, and Motorola. Lumenogic lists Novartis, Siemens, and Corning.

A variation of the prediction market concept is an approach used by Rite-Solutions in which employees are invited to participate in a similar stock market–based game called Mutual Fun. Every person gets an initial $10,000 of hypothetical opinion money to invest in his or her colleagues' ideas. Any player can propose an idea from a cost-saving measure, to a new product, to a new business model. The approach is intended to spur ideas and create a platform for building on them.

Integrated Roadmapping

Roadmapping is the process of compiling a consensus view of the future landscape, along with the timeline-based evolution of products and technologies that get you there. A variety of road maps may emerge from this process, including but not limited to maps for product planning, capability planning, process planning, and integration planning. Most companies have a hodgepodge of road maps (or plans) that are not well connected. When several road maps are aligned strategically, the result is an integrated road map or timeline. Like scenario development, the output of roadmapping describes a plausible future, but the process of getting there is different.

These are the possible steps in developing a road map to support, for example, a company's global growth strategy. The team members may have expertise in or knowledge of the competitive landscape, market drivers and trends, corporate resources and vision, international product and regulatory requirements, operational capabilities, technology trends, and product architecture. Each will provide, on a timeline, general information within his or her area of expertise. This may include anticipated dates for competing product launches, tipping point dates for changes in customer product use, dates when new regulations will be in effect, dates when the company is intending to penetrate specific global markets, and similar factors. Then the group attempts to align all the factors and dates in a way that provides direction for product innovation and/or business model redesign.

The value of the process lies in forcing individuals to articulate their assumptions and in integrating information. As a result, it encourages consensus, contributes to better forecasting, and provides a framework for thinking about the future. The process may uncover promising new technologies, "repurpose" parts from different products and designs, and/or help align technology road maps with suppliers. Motorola, for example, tries to select components and suppliers before design takes place. By developing multiyear technology road maps, that company is able to source suppliers that have the needed capabilities and willingness to invest in technology alignment.

Social Media Options

The growth of Web 2.0 (and 3.0) has provided technological capabilities that did not exist in the past. Increasingly, companies are using social media with both employees and customers to increase collaboration and generate foresight. The virtual platforms enable like-minded individuals both within and external to the firm to share creative ideas as well as perceptions of future trends. Collaboration in communities, responses to blog posts, and contributions to wikis can provide new perspectives. Online contests aimed at fostering innovation help identify ways of co-creating customer value to build into a strategy or business design. Unilever, for example, solicits feedback on ideas and prototypes through two online communities. Its global consumer marketing insights manager Philippa Rose said co-creation would be central for product development as plans for the new variants of Lynx (Axe) planned for 2011 and 2012 both started with co-creation. Dell runs IdeaStorm, a community it launched in 2007 to encourage customers to submit ideas. Michael Dell introduced the concept in a 2007 **YouTube video.**

http://www.youtube.com/watch?v=x66zp6o828U&feature=player_embedded

As of 2010, the community had submitted 14,000 ideas, 4,000 of which were implemented.

Doug Williams in his July 12, 2010, blog post for Forester Research referred to the use of social networks for innovation as "social co-creation" (see Figure 3-3). He presents the concept as both creation or innovation or products and a tool for driving the concepts into the market.

FIGURE 3-3 ➤ Social co-creation

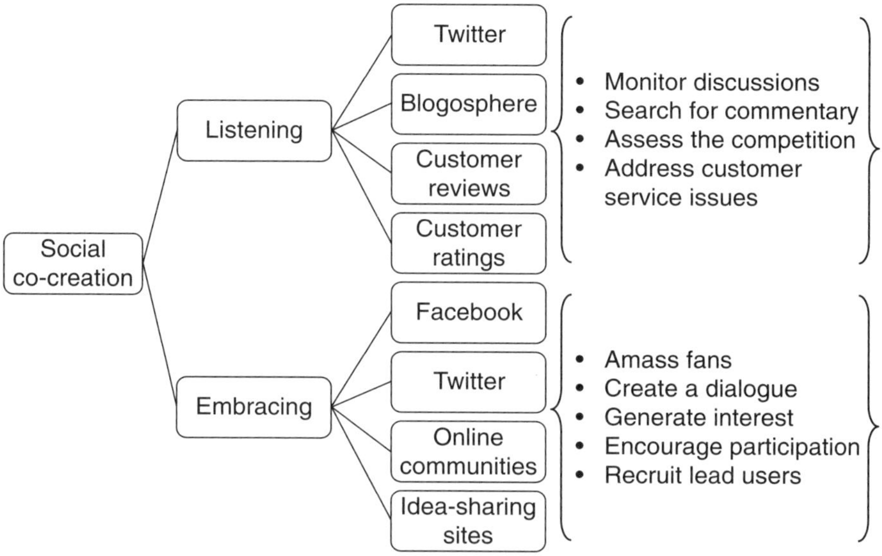

Doug Williams, "Social Co-Creation: 9 Benefits and 6 Challenges for Using Social Technologies to Improve Your Products," blog post, July 12, 2010.

Think about ways in which different social networks might be exploited in terms of better understanding trends, customers, innovation options, and plausible futures.

Facebook: Are new categories of fan pages emerging? Does there appear to be a trend in what types of things people are "liking"?

Twitter: Use search.twitter.com to see what people are talking about that relates to your particular industry or trend interests.

LinkedIn: Use the advanced people search to find potential experts or lead users in your extended industry.

FORESIGHT AND BUSINESS MODELS

It should be clear from this chapter that foresight is a way of thinking. Although there are several tools and processes, they don't provide an absolute description of the future or prove best practices. Use foresight to seek. As Peter Bishop states in his end-of-chapter interview: "Rather than emphasizing accuracy, one should emphasize learning—that the future is a complex, unknown territory that will occur in surprising ways. Competitive advantage is not to predict the future accurately but to learn how it is evolving as quickly as possible and to approach it with all plausible assumptions in play."

PETER BISHOP

THE SIGNIFICANCE OF STRATEGIC FORESIGHT IN THINKING ABOUT THE FUTURE

Dr. Peter Bishop is an associate professor of strategic foresight and director of the graduate program in **futures studies** at the University of

http://www.tech.uh.edu/programs/graduate/futures-studies-in-commerce

Houston. Bishop specializes in techniques for long-term forecasting and planning. He has published a book on the subject, *Thinking about the Future: Guidelines for Strategic Foresight,* with coauthor Andy Hines, and he delivers keynote addresses and conducts seminars on the future for business, government, and not-for-profit organizations. He also facilitates groups in developing scenarios, visions, and strategic plans for the future.

Dr. Peter Bishop
Associate Professor of Strategic Foresight
University of Houston

Peter, many people don't understand what it means to study the future. Can you briefly describe futures studies and explain how you came to be so heavily involved in them?

I had the same reaction when I first came across the program in 1976 while being interviewed for a sociology/statistics position at the University of Houston–Clear Lake. I asked the dean, "What is this program called Studies of the Future?" I was probably somewhat incredulous because I had been socialized as a "scientific sociologist." The dean could be petulant, so he said, "We study the past, don't we? Why can't we study the future?" I had lots of reasons why, but I kept them to myself because I wanted the job!

I taught statistics there for seven or eight years before moving over to the futures program. It was a natural because my interest in sociology was social change.

I did have to readjust some of my assumptions, however, one of which was that scenarios were a cop-out. I wrote a little memo to the other faculty members that they just hadn't done the hard work to support their forecasts with empirical data. I assumed, as most people do today, that you can get pretty good predictions if you collect enough data. I came to the realization shortly thereafter that human systems were actually a radically different type of phenomenon, one in which the normal techniques for scientific predictability don't work. I was okay after that.

So how do we study the future now? The first question I have on a little awareness survey about the future is "Can we know the future?" Many people used to answer yes, but fewer do that today. The better question, however, is "Can we know the futures (plural)?" The answer to that is largely yes, that we can know many, if not most of the plausible futures. That's the result of studying the future: a sense of what futures *might* occur, not which one *will* occur.

The other branch of futures studies is *influencing* the future, not just describing it. That branch includes visioning, planning, and change management, including leadership. Futurists don't do that much differently from other consultants, except that futurists tend to be more long term, more visionary, and more transformational, and they place greater emphasis on broad participation.

In your book* Thinking about the Future *you provide several guidelines for strategic foresight. How is strategic foresight different from other approaches and tools executives typically use in their long-term planning efforts?

As I mentioned, strategic foresight has two major branches: describing what may happen in the world (i.e., forecasting) and influencing that world toward what we want to see happen (i.e., planning). Futurists place more emphasis on what the world is doing in addition to what we will do. The assumption is that the world is not static during the time the plan needs to be implemented and that it contains threats and opportunities that can be used to inform the plan. Any ambitious and long-term plan needs to be successful in a world that will be different from today in important ways, so taking that into account is crucial.

And, as I said, strategic foresight tends to orient the plan toward more ambitious visionary goals that take more time and are more difficult to achieve.

Can you share a few examples of companies that have used strategic foresight as part of their efforts to improve strategies and business models?

Of course, Royal Dutch Shell created important parts of scenario development in the 1970s and continues to use scenarios for its planning. Pharmaceutical companies and healthcare companies in general have used work from the Institute for Alternative Futures a lot. Procter & Gamble uses trend data from the Institute for the Future. My colleague Andy Hines was a resident futurist with the Kellogg Company and Dow Chemical for a time. Kellogg still has a futurist on staff. Other companies that have employed our graduates are Pitney-Bowes, Coca-Cola, Kimberly-Clark, and even Enron, though that didn't prevent its collapse. And I know that Pepsico currently has a major foresight project under way. A number of European companies do a lot of foresight work, such as British Telecom, Nokia, Siemens, and Daimler-Benz.

As you think about the successes and failures you have observed related to business use of the principles of strategic foresight, what key learnings can you share with executives?

I guess the key learning is that you cannot predict the future. We all know that, but we try to do it anyway. So a dose of humility and caution are more important than clarity and certainty. Forecasts are always based on two things: data and assumptions. The data is usually not a problem, but most assumptions about the future have plausible alternatives, each of which leads to an alternative future scenario.

So rather than emphasizing accuracy, one should emphasize learning—that the future is a complex, unknown territory that will occur in surprising ways. Competitive advantage is not to predict the future accurately but to learn how it is evolving as quickly as possible and to approach it with all plausible assumptions in play. So it's a strategic discussion about what is happening and what could happen that promotes understanding more than just information.

On the planning side, it's less about technical processes for achieving goals and more about unleashing the aspirations of the people in the enterprise to make their mark by doing something interesting and valuable.

And the rest is in the book....

REFERENCES

An, Yoonjung, Sungjoo Lee, and Yongtae Park, "Development of an Integrated Product-Service Roadmap with QFD: A Case Study on Mobile Communications," *International Journal of Service Industry Management*, 2008, issue 5, p. 621.

Anders, George, "Business Schools Forgetting Missions?" *Wall Street Journal*, September 26, 2007, p. A2.

Axson, David A., "Scenario Planning: Navigating through Today's Uncertain World," *Journal of Accountancy*, March 2011, pp. 22–29.

Begley, Sharon, "Biologists Hail Dawn of a New Approach: Don't Shoot the Radio," *Wall Street Journal*, February 21, 2003, p. B1.

Borison, Adam, and Gregory Hamm, "Prediction Markets: A New Tool for Strategic Decision Making," *California Management Review*, Summer 2010, pp. 125–141.

Dvorak, Phred, "Best Buy Taps 'Prediction Market,' Imaginary Stocks Let Workers Forecast Whether Retailer's Plans will Meet Goals," *Wall Street Journal*, September 6, 2008. p. B1.

Graefe, Andreas, Stefan Luckner, and Christof Weinhardt, "Prediction Markets for Foresight," *Futures*, May 2010, pp. 394–404.

Hutter, Katja, Julia Hautz, Johann Fuller, Julia Mueller, and Kurt Matzler, "Communitition: The Tension between Competition and Collaboration in Community-Based Design Contests," *Creativity and Innovation Management*, March 2011, pp. 3–21.

LaBarre, Polly, "Provoking the Future," *Harvard Business Review* blog post, July 20, 2011.

Ma, Sai, and Michael Seid, "Using Foresight Methods to Anticipate Future Threats: The Case of Disease Management," *Health Care Management Review*, October–December 2006, pp. 270–279.

Mahanta, Vinod, "Global CEO: Theory of Business Has Changed in the Last Few Years: Paul Laudicinia," *Economic Times* (online), May 21, 2011.

McEleny, Charlotte, "Brands Invest in Online Co-Creation," *New Media Age*, November 18, 2010, p. 1.

Ralston, Bill, "How to Develop a Customized Corporate Energy Strategy," *Strategy and Leadership*, vol. 36, no. 2, 2008, pp. 30–39.

Shell Global Scenarios to 2025, Shell International Limited (SLI), 2005.

Surowiecki, James, *The Wisdom of Crowds*, Anchor, 2005.

Williams, Doug, "Social Co-Creation: 9 Benefits and 6 Challenges for Using Social Technologies to Improve Your Products," blog post, July 12, 2010.

CHAPTER 4

Innovation: Looking for New Beginnings

Perpetual growth requires perpetual renewal, and so innovation is a necessary part of strategies and business models. A persistent environmental scan with an emphasis on foresight may provide the fodder for ongoing innovation. However, there is no single approach to innovation. People generally think about breakthrough, new-to-the-world products as innovations, yet innovations can come incrementally as subtle modifications morph into new products over time and also can be new ways of doing business.

As an example, let's take a look at healthcare. Since at least the introduction of Medicare, a typical business model has been fee for service, encouraging medical providers to increase total services and market share as a means of increasing revenue. However, this model appears to be increasingly unsustainable. The heightened emphasis on patient outcomes, along with financial pressures, healthcare reform, and individual accountability, is puncturing that approach. Thus, business model innovation has been born. Hospitals and health insurers are testing new approaches. Evidence-based protocols, electronic medical systems, and different IT platforms are being examined in an effort to align with physicians and manage services and their related costs. Some of the changes have led to the emergence of retail clinic business models such as MinuteClinic, RediClinic, and Take Care Clinic.

WHAT IS INNOVATION?

Dictionary.com defines innovation as the "introduction of new things or methods." Different experts have categorized innovation in many ways. Many if not most of the categories include variations of incremental, sustaining, transformative, and disruptive innovations. Incremental innovations are those which involve minor changes such as simple product line extensions of the "new and improved" variety. The goal is to help maintain leadership in a particular category. Sustaining innovations tend to maintain a continuous rate of improvement. Some experts consider these types of innovations to be evolutionary in that the difference between the first and last incremental changes can be significant. Both incremental and sustaining innovations are categorized as exploiting known existing capabilities. (Note that the incremental and sustaining approaches were combined into one growth category in Chapter 2 since they are likely to have a lesser impact on business models than is the case for more substantial innovation.)

Transformative and disruptive innovations are more involved with the exploration of new capabilities or technologies. Transformative innovations leverage key assets to provide new value propositions, for example, when a technology commonly used in one industry is applied in an adaptive way in another industry. Disruptive innovations challenge the status quo and may make entire industries obsolete, as in the case of digital photography. Companies could be involved with any or all of these types of innovations.

From a strategy and business model perspective, innovation refers to discovering new ways of creating value for stakeholders, not the least of which are customers. To be able to create value consistently, innovation must be sustainable and ongoing. That means it needs to be a mindset (mental model) of an organization. Although many start-ups can innovate because of their lack of a legacy culture and business approaches, larger organizations ironically find that security and stability are essential to incubate innovation. Companies may need to build a portfolio of business models to accommodate various innovation and growth strategies.

It's human nature to repeat the behaviors that caused past successes. Companies that operate in a stable environment can adopt a static business model with a strategy geared toward predictable changes and continue to be quite successful. Although inertia may set in when the rules of the game are unchallenged for extended periods, success can continue during that time frame. Unfortunately, when circumstances change, the same behaviors may yield different (or no) results. That is when an innovative mindset becomes important.

PRODUCT VERSUS BUSINESS MODEL INNOVATION

Innovation historically has been linked with product development and marketing. As a result, it was driven mostly by R&D, designers, and marketers. Now the focus has shifted to looking for innovations in value chains, business models, and services, and so it increasingly is viewed as a responsibility of the entire organization. Although it is intuitively appealing to have everyone be responsible for innovation, it is hard to make that happen.

New products may be created within an existing business model or may require a new model. As early as 1967, Thomas Robertson described a three-tier framework of (1) continuous innovation, (2) dynamically continuous innovation, and (3) discontinuous innovation. He presented these as a continuum of least to most disruptive in terms of altering established behavior patterns.

I would consider the first to be primarily continuous improvement (e.g., providing better value to customers by reducing variability and waste through techniques such as Six Sigma) or line extensions. Both generally can occur within an existing business model. Dynamically continuous innovation refers to an ongoing approach to new products that goes beyond line extensions. Many of the new products may fit within the firm's current business model, but a few may put some pressure on the status quo. A higher percentage of the product innovations in the third category may require reinventing the business model itself, particularly when a firm is jumping to a new S curve.

Sometimes competitive advantage is built through an innovative business model instead of, or in addition to, new products. Dell's early success in the personal computer (PC) market was due not to a product innovation but to a business model innovation in mass customization. Dell began its business by using a low-cost telesales strategy—bypassing the middlemen—for custom-made PCs. Rather than build state-of-the-art technology, Dell relied on its suppliers to invest in R&D, with Dell focusing primarily on assembly and testing. That enabled the company to have standard, interchangeable parts. Dell built most of its PCs after customers ordered (and often after they paid), without significant mass-produced inventories. Costs were controlled, and cash flow was well managed, with a net positive working capital of seven or eight days. At the time Dell entered this business there was a sufficient number of buyers who were technically competent to configure their own machines and were satisfied with standard (commodity) components. Its brand perception was heavily connected to its high reputation for customer service. The company was quite successful in the innovator and early adopter customer segments, in which the education and hand-holding of value-added resellers was unnecessary.

However, by the early 2000s competitors had begun to close the supply chain advantage of Dell's business model. Dell's ability to maintain its quality and customer-service position was eroding. Consumers increasingly were able to obtain low-cost standard PCs with features close enough to what they would have customized from retail channels. In addition, the industry began facing a number of new trends resulting from a preference for tablet computers and mobile devices as well as a growing interest in cloud computing and complete solutions offerings. The combination of this ecosystem of environmental change is forcing Dell to reexamine both its product strategy and its former business model.

Significant criticism often is lobbed at incumbents that failed to establish new business models when technologies and market shifts (in hindsight) demanded they do so. But the reality is much harder because the timing is uncertain. Digital photography, for example, has been around for decades. When it was in its infancy, customer value was extremely low. Prices were high, quality was erratic, and photo processing was virtually nonexistent. The major players in the industry were understandably reluctant to overinvest in unproven technologies when customers were still deriving value from existing products and services. Kodak did dabble in digital technologies long before it felt the urgency to commit more fully.

Xerox is an example of a company that developed computer products way ahead of their time and ahead of necessary business model changes. During the 1960s, futurists predicted that the office of the future would be paperless if the expected computerization occurred. That posed a threat to Xerox, and so it commissioned a team of computer scientists at its Palo Alto Research Center (PARC) to invent the office of the future. By 1973 the team had created desktop computers that had graphical user interfaces with the ability to use a mouse to drive the cursor and easily make changes. What appeared on the monitor could be printed precisely on the Xerox laser printer. The 100 or so computers at the facility were connected via Ethernet to enable e-mail connections. As indicated in the PBS documentary *The Revenge of the Nerds* (**viewable on YouTube**, from 5:15 to 13:33 minutes), Xerox management was

http://www.youtube.com/watch?v=n1Bg461mnN8

unable to appreciate fully the potential financial value of the innovations the firm owned.

Although in hindsight we can appreciate the significance of the inventions, this would have been a dramatic and risky venture when the traditional Xerox business model was still profitable for copiers. Think about other predictions at the time. Video telephone technology was demonstrated at the World's Fair in the 1960s, but without a critical mass of customers, the value of the innovation was limited. Many people predicted in the 1960s that the United States would be a metric society by the 1990s; it has not happened yet. The QWERTY keyboard designed in the late 1800s to slow down typists to prevent typewriter keys from jamming is still the de facto standard for most computers even though digital reconfiguration could be done easily.

Is there a best practice to adopt here as a solution to the problem? Not really. It's more a matter of mindset. Leaders and managers must be open to the new realities that are developing around them and assess what it would take for them to come to fruition by asking some fundamental questions. At what rate is it likely that customers will adopt the new technologies or approaches embedded in the product innovation? What will it take for a complete solution to exist? Can the company provide the complete solution, or is it necessary to establish strategic alliances and partnerships? Is it better to launch the new product incrementally, allowing time for customers to adapt? Can the new product be developed with the systems, resources, competencies, and culture of the current business system, or will a transformed business model be necessary? Can the firm function with two different business models (perhaps as different business units), or will a complete transition be required? How can the firm create value for both the customers and the company?

DIFFUSION OF INNOVATION

Part of the answer lies in the concept of diffusion of innovation, which is the adoption of a new product by the market or a new technology across society. The concept, first introduced by the sociologist Everett Rogers in the 1960s, spawned the traditional bell-shaped innovation life cycle curve, also known as the innovation diffusion model (see Figure 4-1). The theory holds that the first customers to use a truly new product are innovators, the small percentage of individuals (or sometimes organizations) who are venturesome and willing to take the risk of the new product or technology.

The next category of customers consists of early adopters who benefit from the experience of the innovators to help make their own decisions. This group often consists of opinion leaders (or what Malcolm Gladwell refers to as *connectors* in *The Tipping Point*). Assuming the innovators and early adopters have positive experiences with the innovation, there will be a snowball effect or bandwagon effect as it is adopted by the early majority and late majority. The last customers who adopt the concept are referred to as laggards.

Note that this curve is more appropriate for new-to-the-world innovations than for imitative new products. During the introduction phase, one or a few companies are producing and selling the products. If there is a successful

FIGURE 4-1 ➤ Innovation diffusion model

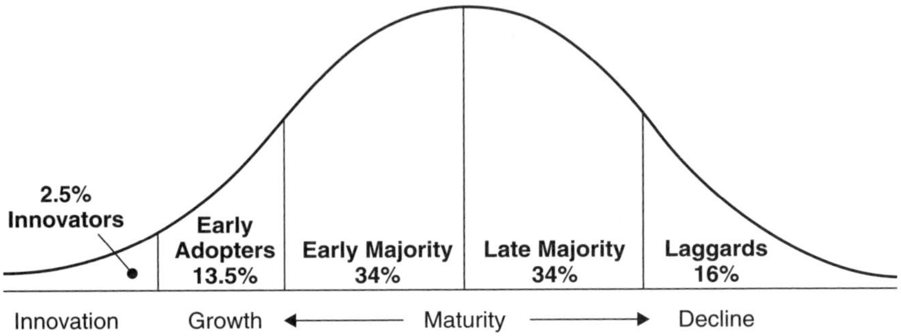

Source: Everett Rogers.

introduction phase, the existing sellers have demonstrated the potential value of the new offering, attracting new competitors into the field in the growth phase. During this phase the rate of adoption increases as several competitors share the burden of educating the market. As the size of the market continues to grow into maturity, sellers begin to compete on the basis of differential positioning.

Diffusion of innovation is neither uniform nor inevitable. Products that require substantial behavioral change on the part of customers (e.g., converting to a non-QWERTY keyboard) or have significant switching costs (e.g., when a firm has to replace all inventoried consumables to be able to use a new piece of equipment) will take longer to achieve market penetration or may not move beyond the introduction phase. That begs the question of whether there is really a first-mover advantage.

This is a question that commonly is argued on both sides by businesses. Proponents state that first movers establish a dominant position, giving them an advantage over new entrants. However, the *remembered* first mover is often the first *successful* firm in the market that has learned from the mistakes of prior unsuccessful entrants of which we are unaware. Therefore, the first company associated with a particular innovation may be considered the de facto first mover. As was mentioned in Chapter 1, even though Apple is considered by many to have had a first-mover advantage with its iPod, it benefited from prior MP3 manufacturers, the experiences of Napster, and improved data transfer resulting from broadband. Friendster and MySpace preceded Facebook. Numerous attempts at video telephony preceded Skype and video mobile.

That is why the classic model is flawed. It is very common for a new product category to start, experience a stall (or chasm), and then either collapse or become successful after getting beyond the chasm. (Also, the successful

FIGURE 4-2 ➤ The innovation chasm

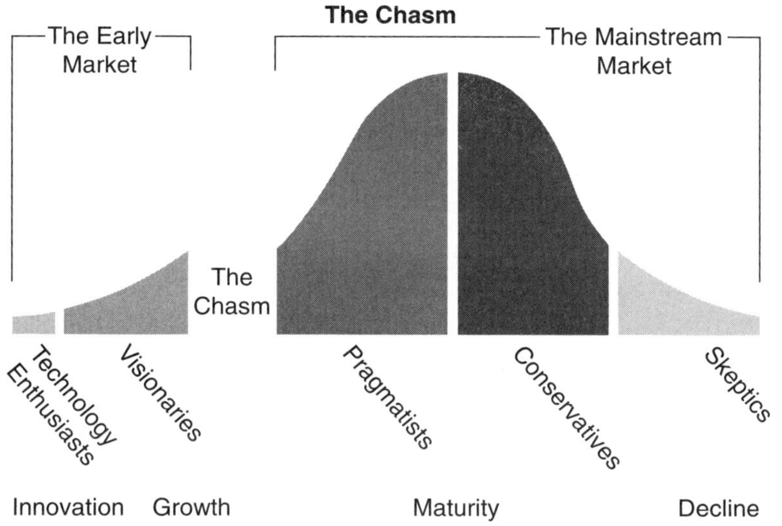

product may or may not be the one that created the category.) Geoffrey Moore described that phenomenon from a technology perspective in *Crossing the Chasm*. His categories are shown in Figure 4-2. The chasm represents the gap between sales to what he termed enthusiasts and visionaries and sales to the rest of the market.

Of course, many new products are not innovations in the sense of starting a new product category. Most are launched into an existing product market with the goal of differentiation rather than invention. According to conventional wisdom in the pharmaceutical industry, a new brand has 120 days after launch to create momentum. Therefore, companies must establish a clear value proposition for all relevant stakeholders during the prelaunch period. Patients who purchase the product in pharmacies are looking for relief from an ailment. Managed care professionals purchasing the product for in-hospital use are concerned with reimbursement issues. Physicians purchasing the product for use in clinics want relief from paperwork and clear proof of efficacy. Value and benefits have to be expressed in terms relevant to those particular audiences.

Similar concepts of segmented brand value can apply to other products as well. Tools aimed at do-it-yourselfers versus professional contractors need to address different levels of competency, price sensitivity, and channel even if the product is essentially the same. Products being launched into different countries must be glocalized to meet specific value requirements. The roles of users, decision makers, payers, channel members, and other influencers have to be considered as well.

The point here is again the wisdom of and. In light of the incredible importance of innovation in products and business models, the challenge of predicting one absolute future, and the risk of inertia once success is achieved, portfolio thinking is increasingly important. Companies must establish continual flows of innovation and build an adaptable culture to turn those innovations into realities. Innovation on existing products usually can be done within the existing business model, whereas innovation involving the creation of new product categories may require business model adaptation.

INNOVATING EXISTING PRODUCT LINES

Most products will die if they are not reinvented as the marketplace changes. Since consumers now cook less (reducing the amount of aluminum foil and plastic wrap used), Reynolds and Glad Wrap introduced line extensions to revive their products. Reynolds discovered that one of the biggest complaints customers had about aluminum foil was that it stuck to food. That research led to Reynolds Release, the first variation of the product since 1947, causing an increase in use. Clorox found that its Glad plastic wrap did not provide the leakproof seal that consumers wanted and soon launched Press 'n Seal.

Extending a franchise offers a number of benefits that new-to-the-world new product development does not. The major benefit is that extension capitalizes on the company's most important assets: its brand names. Thus, the company moves into a new category from a position of strength. A further benefit is that the investment outlays typically necessary to establish a new brand—a significant expense—are minimal. However, line extensions must offer new value to customers. Companies that are successful at line extensions tend to rotate the brand assignments of their product managers regularly to prevent them from getting stuck in ruts. This reduces the likelihood of proliferating virtually identical products.

A consumer is exposed to hundreds of brand names every day. Being a well-known brand is not sufficient to be a good brand extension. Few consumers want JELL-O shoelaces or Tide frozen entrees. A brand can be extended successfully to a new category when it has both fit and leverage. Fit is when the consumer accepts the new product as logical and would expect it from the brand. Leverage is when consumers, simply by knowing the brand, can think of important ways in which they perceive the new brand extension would be better than competing products in the category.

Since a brand's meaning can change over time as brand extensions are introduced, management needs to develop a brand plan: which extensions are introduced in the short term and which others become possible in the long term. One must develop a long-term scenario to avoid diluting important elements of the brand and improve the odds of pursuing more remote areas where the brand could have leverage.

CONTINUAL IDEA SOURCES

Different innovations relate to different perspectives on customer needs. Some innovations (primarily incremental and sustaining) focus on continuous improvement in satisfying known customer needs. Some focus on satisfying existing but previously unarticulated needs. Others dramatically alter the ways needs are satisfied. Still others may redefine an entire need category. Although there are many approaches to doing customer research to support these innovations, incremental innovations are more apt to use traditional research, whereas the others use a host of other techniques.

Companies often can discover how to improve their ability to address current needs through surveys and focus groups consisting of "typical" customers. This is particularly useful for products in established markets that are still growing. Customers can indicate whether a product should be longer or shorter, heavier or lighter, or sharper or duller. The resulting innovations are generally incremental and can be accomplished within the existing business model. However, there are situations in which even a well-defined need may be addressed more rapidly through open innovation, enabling a product to be brought to market sooner.

Open innovation, a concept pioneered by **Henry Chesbrough,** refers to the

http://www.youtube.com/watch?v=2UDBaDtwXfI

process of seeking solutions to identified problems by reaching out to people and organizations beyond the firm's employees. Several organizations have emerged over the last decade that enable companies with technical or scientific product challenges to find potential solutions from external parties. NineSigma helps its clients prepare technical briefs and find people who can solve the identified technical challenges (this is somewhat analogous to the approach used by headhunters to find appropriate job candidates). InnoCentive posts scientific challenges from its seeker clients and pays solvers a monetary award for a workable solution. YourEncore is composed of retired scientists and engineers who can work with clients on specific short-term innovation assignments. yet2 acts as a channel to acquire, license, and/or sell unused patents. Still other potential contributors to this process are InnovationXchange and Planet Eureka.

The intent of open innovation is to leverage the external sources of technology and innovation to contribute a solution to a part of a product you are developing or occasionally to provide the complete product solution. During the last decade Procter & Gamble has made a concerted effort to increase the percentage of products with elements that originated from outside the company. In fact, it renamed its R&D group C&D for "connect and develop." Although some of the connections occur as a result of current interpersonal networks, there are several companies that can facilitate the process.

Access to an expanded pool of ideas through open innovation can be very appealing, but there are potential downsides. Intellectual property ownership has to be carefully evaluated and managed. Trust has to be built on both sides, and it can't exist if there is a "not-invented-here" negative cultural bias. Also, it takes time to build the open innovation network. Thus, this is not a quick fix, and managers must decide if and how to integrate it into their business model.

Companies using online communities to generate product improvement ideas should be prepared to receive many incomplete and irrelevant ideas along with a few nuggets of knowledge. Because of the potential volume of submissions, companies are well advised to make their questions clearly focused (e.g., asking about a specific feature or technology) or closed-ended (multiple choice or ratings). This enables faster quantitative evaluation that is useful for line extensions and continuous improvement of products.

It may be harder to develop innovations for needs that customers cannot articulate. When working on breakthrough new products, companies routinely overestimate the value to the market and/or the speed of the product's acceptance. Open innovation is useful here as well. Cocreation is a variant of open innovation by which companies create products along with their customers. The most explicit example is perhaps Facebook, for which the company provides the platform and individual customers create their own unique products and user experiences.

Procter & Gamble, in contrast, is interested in both innovations and improvements to existing products and marketing strategies. In April 2005 it instituted its first annual "consumer is boss" event to solicit new product ideas. One idea from a seven-year-old girl was to have consumers vote for the next flavor of Crest. As a result, the company had a web vote to select between lemon, berry, and tropical fruit flavors to extend Crest Whitening Expressions.

The Iams managers at P&G learned that some pet owners added treats (table scraps) to their dry dog food to induce older pets to eat it. Follow-up quantitative research revealed that 40 percent of owners used such methods, and so the brand launched Savory as a more nutritious alternative to table scraps.

Although multiple approaches can be used, managers should continually challenge themselves to focus on *why* people do the things they do—and the relevant competition at those times—and use the information in product development and marketing. Clayton Christensen, author of *The Innovator's Solution*, suggests that the reason many products fail is that managers don't look at markets the way customers experience life. For example, when the managers of a fast-food chain wanted to improve the firm's milk shake sales and profits, they first asked customers whether the shakes should be thicker, be chunkier, or have different flavors. They made the changes requested by customers, but nothing happened. When they brought in another group of researchers, it was discovered that most of the customers consumed shakes to make a long, boring commute easier. Since it could take 20 minutes to sip the shake through a thick straw, it relieved the boredom of the trip. The competition was not just other shakes but also "boredom, bagels, bananas, doughnuts, instant breakfast drinks and, possibly, coffee." The new perspective changed the new product concepts.

Qualitative techniques such as ethnography and customer visit programs, as well as lead user research, can play an important role in identifying unarticulated needs. Ethnography refers to observational research that captures insights within the context of the customer's realities. Gerry Katz, executive vice president of Applied Marketing Science, Inc., has an interesting four-minute YouTube video describing the use of **ethnography** or observational

http://www.youtube.com/watch?v=9tHgNXzS2EY

research. In this primer he describes how an observational study of nurses using dialysis machines uncovered an unarticulated need that was converted into a highly successful product feature.

That is why ethnography can be such a useful tool. Ethnography can contribute to a better voice of the customer for new products. Not only do product developers observe customers, they also consider the needs of various other influencers in the purchase decision. IDEO, a design consulting firm in California, has a YouTube video describing its **"deep dive" approach** to http://www.youtube.com/watch?v=M66ZU2PCIcM

product innovation. In this video they redesign a shopping cart by studying how people use carts in stores, gathering statistics on the risk of child injuries, and talking to retail owners and security personnel.

Customer visit programs provide another approach to ethnography that is most commonly used in business-to-business (B2B) situations. A cross-functional group is selected to visit a customer site to observe a product (e.g., factory automation) being used. The group may consist of engineers, technicians, and sales and marketing personnel in an attempt to uncover unarticulated needs from a variety of perspectives.

Lead user research, championed by Professor Eric von Hippel from the MIT Sloan School of Management, focuses on gathering ideas from people or industries that already are solving problems you are grappling with. For example, von Hippel explained how the automotive industry obtained several ideas for anti-lock brakes from the aerospace industry. His website **http:// www.leaduser.com**

http://www.leaduser.com

contains several videos describing the process of lead user innovation.

Lead users—companies or individuals with more extreme or demanding needs for a product—are important sources of innovative product ideas. More representative customers provide more input for line extensions, concept development, and life cycle sales forecasts. However, all contribute the voice of the customer to new product development projects.

Toshiba America Medical Systems has developed strong relationships with leading U.S. medical institutions to gain a better understanding of the market opportunity for medical imaging products. It took advantage of a physician advocate and ally at Johns Hopkins to establish a group of thought leaders and leading medical experts. The team was invited to sit on Toshiba's advisory board, reviewing beta products and pushing innovation.

GE Healthcare encourages an active involvement of lead users, who are referred to as luminaries. Most are well-published doctors and research scientists from leading medical institutions. GE brings them together for regular "medical advisory board sessions" to assess the evolution of GE technology.

FIGURE 4-3 ➤ Customer value chain

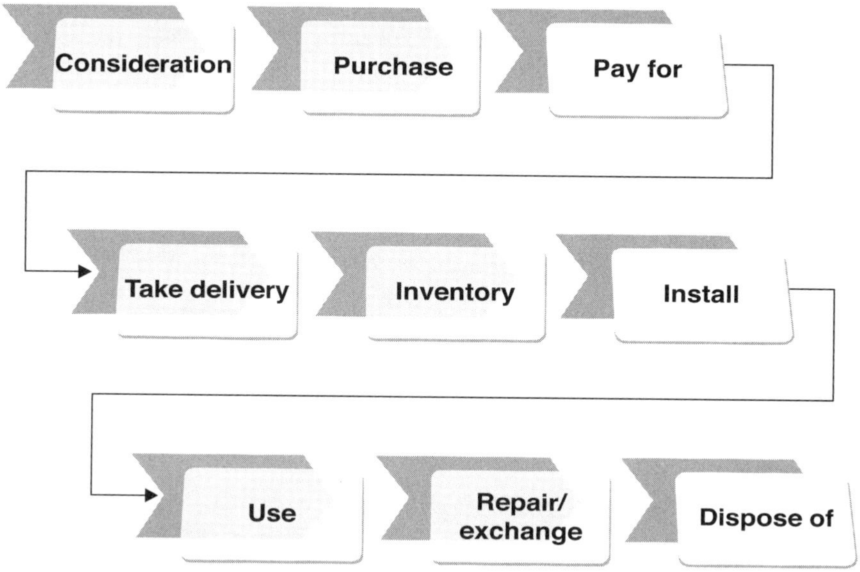

Sometimes the needs are not product-specific but instead deal with broader business issues such as channels to market or improvements in the customer value chain. Use qualitative research to probe ways in which customers might gain more value from interacting with your business, starting with each touch point of the customer value chain (CVC). Map your firm's CVC (Figure 4-3) and then look for opportunities to improve the total value experience.

Here are some questions related to each touch point that may generate innovative ideas for customer value enhancement:

- Prepurchase education and information during the consideration stage can provide value—especially for complex decisions—by helping customers find the best fit for their goals and needs. Demonstrations, trials, and white papers can increase comfort in the purchase decision. Research ways to innovate the education process, for example.
- Streamlining the purchase through simpler paperwork or easier payment terms will increase the value quotient for some customers. Probe customers' level of satisfaction with the purchase process.
- Simplifying payment through techniques such as pay at the pump (for gas), fewer hidden fees, and smartphone transactions may enhance value. Examine the potential for innovative applications of technology.

- Delivery on the customer's terms (using, for example, straightforward appointments, drop shipping, or expediting) may generate value. Look for potential delivery problems to solve.
- The availability of or access to inventory, perhaps as a result of convenient distributor locations or on-site inventory with pay-as-you-go contracts, can shift preference from one supplier to another. Assess how time-sensitive the customer need is.
- Installation can be another area in which to rethink value. Are there opportunities to add custom installation to a do-it-yourself product or vice versa? Identify customer installation frustrations.
- Can value be added at the usage stage by reducing features (to make it simpler) or adding features (to enhance capabilities)? This is an area where ethnography and customer visit programs can yield insights.
- Are repair services valued? Can you increase value at this point, similar to Best Buy's Geek Squad? Test different service packages with customers.
- Do customers value the ability to return, exchange, or upgrade the product? Is it possible to add value there?
- With growing concerns about ecofriendliness, is there a value opportunity in reducing the end-of-life impact either with environmentally friendly components or through a solid recycling program?

As you research these touch points, think about what the results might require in terms of business model changes so that you are able to establish and maintain a competitive advantage. Do you have the right structure, sufficient capabilities, and a supporting culture?

A related consideration is whether customers can obtain a complete solution from your company or whether there are missing complements. Note that when Apple launched iPod, part of its success was contingent on the existence of iTunes stores. Because of the contracts Apple had with record labels, as well as the enabling technology of broadband connectivity, customers were able to obtain a more complete solution than they would have if they'd had only access to the purchase of the core product.

Innovations rooted in the latest technology may or may not have a market application, but they cannot be ignored. Sometimes a new technology can make obsolete (or at a minimum partially replace) an existing technology, as we have seen with digital video streaming, mobile communication applications, and Web 3.0. In other situations, technology may enable increased customer value through cost reductions or enhanced convenience even if the core product is essentially the same.

BUSINESS CASE KNOWLEDGE

An innovative culture is more than creative; it's also pragmatic. That is why companies really interested in driving innovation from a business perspective understand the need to train employees on business issues such as developing a business case for new products.

It's important to approach case building as ammunition for decision making. It starts with gathering data on market potential, realistically assessing which factors might make it easier or harder for the product to gain market acceptance, and then forecasting accordingly. In other words, the business case should predict the *outcome* if this decision is taken. Determine reasonable cash flow projections with rough probabilities of achieving various cash flows during an acceptable payback period.

Beyond the forecast revenues and costs, there may be soft benefits to consider, including increased brand awareness, referrals, and higher customer satisfaction. Although soft benefits cannot be translated directly into hard dollars and cents, they can be linked with carefully articulated assumptions. For example, if the assumption is that a new product will prevent defection to the competition, the financial value of this business can be estimated.

The business case is a skeleton plan that provides the financial, competitive, and market justification for a project. It is essentially an economic proposal for an investment and should build from data. It is sometimes helpful to think of a business case in the context of an entrepreneur compiling a business plan in an effort to get venture capital. Since the quality of a business case can have a direct impact on making correct decisions about the acceptance or rejection of a product concept, it's worth doing right. That doesn't mean simply following a best-practice template to give you an answer magically. Rather, it means objectively evaluating the positives and negatives of the concept for the organization. It also may require explaining why other concepts were rejected in favor of this one.

The process of developing the business case begins with answering the question of why you are considering this concept at this time. Carefully consider its fit with the business strategy, product strategy, and/or product road map. Is this a proactive or reactive product? Will it fill a gap or open new opportunities? What is the size of the opportunity and the expected financial performance? Is the concept manufacturable, and do we have the capabilities to do it? What might be the consequences of not pursuing this concept? What are the risks, and how will they be mitigated? Don't assume that the answers to all these questions are obvious. They may not be.

INGRAINING AN INNOVATIVE CULTURE

Anyone actively involved in product development is aware that ideation is just the beginning of the process. In addition to knowledge about business case writing, there is a lot of work to be done to move the idea through development to ultimate commercialization. It is these latter steps in the process that are the most time-consuming and prone to error.

The same thing can be said about innovating a business model. It's not simply an awareness that a potential new S curve is emerging. That may generate some ideas about how to compete, but until managers think through the resources, competencies, structure, and organizational culture required to make that business model real, it's just a daydream.

Companies have experimented with programs and initiatives to build an innovative culture in their organizations. Innovation fairs, online forums, brown-bag lunches, suggestion boxes, and other approaches have been attempted. *USA Today* recently posted an article about AOL's effort to create an innovative culture by changing the firm's workspace and inviting more playfulness, such as encouraging employees to write on the walls and play pool and Ping-Pong. Although there is nothing wrong with creating the right environment for creativity, it is insufficient in itself as a tool to change culture.

These brainstorming events are valuable when they generate excitement and involve a broad cross section of the organization. Unfortunately, they can be demotivating if employees receive no feedback on their ideas and feel they were not heard. Even with careful positioning of the ideation event and consistent follow-up to contributors, these tools are not enough to ingrain innovation in a culture. Part of the problem is that these are temporary measures that don't necessarily address the core cultural issues. Innovation success has to be woven into the fabric of the organization, and employees need to know what problems they are being challenged to explore and the types of questions they should be asking.

People prosper from success. Help employees, especially those early in their careers, recognize the various aspects of innovation and motivate performance in that direction. Motivation does not have to be financial; intrinsic motivators such as involvement, status, and acknowledgment can be highly effective. Assign them to successful work groups or mentors so they can experience vicarious innovation success. When possible, allow (or encourage) employees to help implement the innovative ideas they generated. Create an environment that enables institutionalizing innovation, even if it takes time. Jeff Bezos, CEO of Amazon.com, suggests that it takes five to seven years before a modification to its business model can take root.

People need to be on the lookout for changes to the basis of competition. Are customers beginning to obtain the functionality you provide in ways not offered by you (or offered by organizations that were previously indirect competition)? Although Netflix and Blockbuster were competitors in the video rental business, Netflix launched its DVD rental-by-mail business in 1998 as a different business model from Blockbuster's brick-and-mortar approach. When Blockbuster matched the mail-order strategy, Netflix added online streaming. Then, in early 2011, kiosk vendors, led by Redbox, generated more DVD transactions than traditional video stores. As customer purchase behavior shifted, Blockbuster faced dual competition from Netflix and Redbox, causing stress on its business model. Blockbuster was later acquired by Dish Network LLC.

All employees play a vital role in detecting market shifts, but whereas some executives excel at managing an ongoing business, the more entrepreneurial-minded ones are needed to question the status quo. Be sure both types of talent are present in the organization and be prepared to tap into the appropriate performers as circumstances dictate. Build in time for strategic thinking in the organization and make it clear what the focus of innovation efforts should be. Employees can contribute more successfully when they know the boundaries of the desired innovations.

Nokia Group, for example, focuses its innovation efforts by "studying user needs, emerging technologies and the changing business environment within the mobility and communications space." Because new ideas are limited to these customer-need categories, extraneous pursuits are minimized. Similarly, Air Liquide shifted focus from product innovation to what it termed demand innovation, meeting existing demand in a new way. As a supplier of industrial gases to the pulp and paper industry, the firm saw its income drop as the product became a commodity in the 1990s. After unsuccessfully investing R&D resources in an ozone-friendly alternative to bleach for paper and pulp, the company discovered a need for gas-management services.

P&G encourages innovation through cross-pollination from one product to another rather than inventing from scratch. Tide StainBrush, an electric device for removing stains from clothing, uses the same basic mechanism as Crest Spinbrush Pro toothpaste. They also encourage thinking in terms of generating more solutions to customer needs rather than in terms of extending products. P&G gained a greater "share of mouth" with its Spinbrush and Whitestrips.

Numerous articles have described various components of 3M's approach to building an innovative culture. From a technical perspective, the company has a database of reports written by its more than 7,000 scientists, but its culture of collaboration is cited most often as its secret weapon. It has support networks, such as an employee-run Tech Forum that organizes events to stimulate thinking and interaction. Collaboration is built into the employee evaluation system.

Employees are allowed to spend 15 percent of their time on pet projects, and 3M even provides innovation funds, which it calls Genesis Grants, that can be used for projects that don't fit neatly into existing structures.

Although senior leaders may work on building new business models on the basis of their analysis of the strategic environment, innovation also can come from within as employees identify potentially new product and revenue streams that don't fit inside an existing business model. Management should enhance the culture by validating innovative behavior each day and by encouraging open communication. Only by empowering creativity in the workforce will companies be able to move beyond the status quo.

DAVE FRANCHINO

INNOVATION FROM THE CONTEXT OF BUSINESS MODELS

Dave Franchino is president and principal of Design Concepts, Inc., a product innovation consultancy that specializes in helping clients build brands and business through product strategy, research, human factors, design, engineering, and prototyping. Drawing on nearly 25 years of diverse experiences as a manger in a Fortune 50 business, a small business owner, an entrepreneur, and a consultant, Dave coaches and mentors clients on creating world-class business and design solutions with true impact. He can be reached at dave.franchino@design-concepts.com.

Dave Franchino
President and Principal
Design Concepts, Inc.

Dave, many (but not all) business model transformations occur around new products and services. What are some of the techniques you use at Design Concepts to innovate new products to help companies meet their growth objectives?

Perhaps one of the most powerful techniques for creating new business models is to allow new product development teams to set aside preconceived notions of what or where the solution lies, at least at the beginning of a new initiative. If you begin a development project assuming that the solution will be a specific product, odds are that that's where you'll end up. Instead, we encourage our clients to embrace a "discovery" process at the onset of any new strategic initiative. If you have the courage to allow teams to freely explore what your customers are truly seeking, often you'll find solutions which involve new ways of extracting value from the marketplace.

During this discovery phase, we are collectively looking for inspiration from three different and important avenues.

First, we look at what's happening in what we call the *strategic ecosystem*. This is the relevant context or environment in which the business opportunity is operating. What are competitors doing? Are there any relevant changes in government regulations? Are there societal or cultural trends which can impact the business? Are there emerging technologies that are likely to have an influence? Are there new ways in which money is being spent in this general area? A relevant and current example of changes in this type of ecosystem would be recent regulations, trends, and technologies in sustainability and environmental consciousness which can create both strategic opportunities and threats if not thoughtfully studied and considered. There are certainly new business models that are emerging due to changes in this area!

Second, we want to make sure the clients we work with fully study and understand the prevailing environment and relevant cultural issues within their own firms. Aside from what's happening externally, factors within a company can create significant opportunity, or headwinds, for new business models. What are current corporate competitive strengths? What are overall strategic opportunities? What is the appetite for innovation? What internal barriers might exist, including capital, timing, and even cultural resistance? This is particularly crucial for new business models since tinkering with the way in which a firm makes money is perhaps one of the most complex and riskiest forms of innovation.

Third, we want to make sure we study the users of products and services in the area of interest. We don't just mean consumers but rather decision makers who impact selection or purchase, influencers who might be thought leaders or sway opinions on use, and actual users who will engage with the product or service direction. To the extent practical, we'll recommend using direct, ethnographic, observational research to immerse our team in the lives, minds, and hearts of these users.

If one looks thoughtfully at the context, company, and users, without a preconceived notion of a specific solution, new business model opportunities can emerge from a variety of areas. We had one client who was looking to develop a new version of a medical diagnostic meter and instead determined there was a far more significant revenue opportunity helping its customers manage documents and control the data created by the meters. What started as a product initiative became a new data management service. This type of perspective-changing realization can drive significant growth opportunities in unexpected areas, but it requires having the flexibility and courage to allow teams to look beyond traditional or expected solutions.

How do some of the concepts of product innovation translate to business model innovation?

Actually, a really important perspective used in product innovation called design thinking is based on the fact that product innovation concepts and methods can be used to attack a much broader range of business issues. In particular, business model innovation is a tremendous area in which to use some of the same techniques. If you look at the front-end basics of any thoughtful product design process, they're going to include some period of discovery research to establish context, some period of conceptualization to envision future scenarios, and some level of rapid prototyping and testing.

In my opinion, these are areas within the design process that translate directly to the redefinition of business models. Lately, I have been particularly fascinated by efforts to prototype new business models. Although prototyping is a concept generally associated with products or services, with a bit of creativity, it is possible to prototype, test, evaluate, and refine a new business model, often on a smaller scale, in localized markets or with certain aspects simulated. Just as with new products and services, prototyping can identify business model problems, suggest refinements, and tailor solutions without risking the tremendous time and capital necessary for full-scale implementation.

Do you think business model transformation is the result of or a catalyst for product innovation?

It's going to sound cliché, but I think it can be a bit of both. Take everyone's favorite example, the iPod. MP3 players had been around for years, but the real innovation here was the adaptation and inclusion of iTunes—certainly an entirely new business model for what had traditionally been a hardware company. Likewise, Amazon needed to be innovative in creating a new product—the Kindle—before they could realize the business model that could result from a new format for written words.

I think this topic is particularly rich in today's connected world as the boundaries between products and services blur and new business models emerge, both requiring and creating the need for new products. If anything, the pace of transformation is only going to accelerate. The next decade is going to see some significant opportunities and challenges for traditional business models in telecommunications, healthcare, information technology, transportation, and so forth. And it's not just new or high-technology businesses. Agricultural product companies are into the information and commodities business. Banks have become investment firms.

I think it benefits a company to truly challenge itself to think of ways it can leverage a deep understanding of one aspect of the user's experience into new ways to add value *and* make money.

Many companies apply sophisticated processes such as DMAIC [define, measure, analyze, improve, control] to manage the change to a new business model. Do you think the Six Sigma framework is appropriate for significant business model change or more for incremental change?

I think, in theory, Six Sigma can provide a powerful framework and methodology for identifying and controlling change—even business model change—but I've found the reality often falls short of the potential. The problem isn't in the methodology per se but rather in human nature and the way in which many firms have implemented Six Sigma. At its core, DMAIC is all about careful definition, control, analysis, analytics, and risk reduction. An almost inevitable result is that Six Sigma processes will put a tremendous premium on eliminating ambiguity and unknowns. But implementing new business models is fraught with ambiguity, intuition, and gut feel—almost by definition. An overly rigid implementation of Six Sigma can mean promising alternatives are cast aside by well-intentioned staff seeking to reduce perceived risk. Ironically, continuing to do that which is well described and known can often be the riskiest path of all. What I like to see are companies that can combine the ambiguity of fuzzy front end design thinking—and all the intuition that entails—with the rigor and structure of a Six Sigma process. As I mentioned earlier, if you can find a way to use rapid prototyping on your business model, you can reduce the costs and the fear of failure and encourage more of a risk-taking environment. Simply recognizing both the power and the pitfalls of a DMAIC process can allow companies to leverage these methods most effectively in their search for new business models.

In your opinion, are resilient, innovative cultures more receptive to business model change initiatives?

Absolutely! Companies that are tinkering with their business model need to be flexible, nimble, and resilient. There are going to be missteps and necessary adjustments, refinements, and evolutions. But I've found that the most innovative cultures can encourage a degree of introspection, creativity, and risk taking that allows new concepts and methods to flourish. I think this is particularly important because the competitive free market will, by design, seek to commoditize any product or service over time. Often, however, as one aspect of a market is commoditized by competition, there are entirely new and even more lucrative business models created by expanding your definition of how you add value for your customers.

Can you think of examples of companies that have been successful in transitioning to innovative business models?

Well, it's hardly a surprise, but I think my favorite example is IBM. In 1992, only 11 percent of IBM's revenue came from providing services. The M in IBM certainly stood for machines, and a look through their annual reports provides almost no mention of services other than the observation that they weren't particularly profitable! A simple statement in their 1994 annual report challenged their leadership to consider "realigning the way we deliver value to customers." By 2008, that realignment meant that almost 60 percent of their revenue came from services. At the time, this transition was tremendously innovative. And what is most remarkable to me is that this increase wasn't simply a reflection of a drop in revenue from hardware and software. It predominantly represented *new* business for IBM—a new business model upon which the entire future of the company was built.

There are plenty of other great examples. Disney was once a cartoon company and now makes its money from a remarkably diverse set of business models.

Any final words of wisdom related to business model innovation?

I'd just offer up both a cautionary tale and some encouraging words. Innovating the way in which you make money can be among the most difficult types of innovation to pursue. The problem is that business models are typically ingrained deep in the DNA of a firm, and the bigger and more complex the firm, the more ingrained and intractable the inertia around that business model. Just in the last year we've seen the demise of Borders and the bankruptcy/

sale of Blockbuster, two firms that were unable to revise their business models to suit a changing competitive landscape. There is an encouraging point to this risk, though. I have found that in general, no matter how the landscape for your business changes, there are usually ways to morph and alter your business model to leverage your competence and expertise and remain relevant. The best companies have found ways to do this, and both their product offerings and their business models often bear little resemblance to what they looked like originally. By leveraging the tools and methods used for product and service innovation, I think firms can think of novel new ways to both add and extract value.

REFERENCES

Birkinshaw, Julian, Cyril Bouquet, and J.-L. Barsoux, "The 5 Myths of Innovation," *MIT Sloan Management Review*, Winter 2011, pp. 43–50.

"Business: The Rise of the Creative Consumer: The Future of Innovation," *The Economist*, March 12, 2005, p. 75.

Byrnes, Nanette, Robert Berner, Wendy Zellner, and William C. Symonds, "Branding: Five New Lessons," *BusinessWeek*, February 14, 2005, pp. 26–28.

Christensen, Clayton M., and Michael E. Raynor, "Creating a Killer Product," *Forbes*, October 13, 2003, p. 82.

Colvin, Geoff, "Here It Is Now, You Design It!" *Fortune*, May 26, 2008, p. 34.

Gladwell, Malcolm, *The Tipping Point*, Little Brown, 2000.

Graham, Jefferson, "AOL Soaks Up Silicon Valley Spirit To Inspire New Apps," USAToday.com, June 28, 2011.

Gruenwedel, Erik, "Dish Network Buys Blockbuster: Now What?" *Home Media Magazine*, April 11–17, 2011, p. 1.

"Innovate or Die," *Strategic Direction*, July 2011, pp. 12–14.

Jaruzelski, Barry, and Richard Holman, "Casting a Wide Net: Building the Capabilities for Open Innovation," *Ivey Business Journal* online, March–April 2011.

Kaufman, Kenneth, "A New Business Model for Hospitals," *Trustee*, May 2010, pp. 14–18.

Kelley, Braden, "DMAIC for Innovation," *Blogging Innovation*, June 27, 2011.

MacVaugh, Jason, and Francesco Schiavone, "Limits to the Diffusion of Innovation," *European Journal of Innovation Management*, Summer 2010, pp. 197–221.

Maynard, Micheline, "Wrapping a Familiar Name around a New Product," *New York Times*, May 22, 2004, p. C1.

Neff, Jack, "P&G Kisses Up to the Boss: Consumers," *Advertising Age*, May 2, 2005, p. 18.

Nunes, Paul, and Tim Breene, "Reinvent Your Business before It's Too Late," *Harvard Business Review*, January–February 2011, pp. 80–87.

Robertson, Thomas S., "The Process of Innovation and the Diffusion of Innovation," *Journal of Marketing*, January 1967, pp. 14–19.

Roche, Eileen, "Product Development: Why Line Extensions Often Backfire," *Harvard Business Review*, March–April 1999, pp. 19–21.

Scanlon, Jessie, "How 3M Encourages Collaboration," Businessweek.com, September 2, 2009.

"Special Report: Don't Laugh at Gilded Butterflies," *The Economist*, April 24, 2004, p. 81.

Tauber, Edward M., "Brand Leverage: Strategy for Growth in a Cost-Control World," *Journal of Advertising Research*, August–September 1988, p. 28.

Teresko, John, "P&G's Secret: Innovating Innovation," *Industry Week*, December 2004, pp. 26–32.

Välikangas, Liisa, and Michael Gibbert, "Boundary-Setting Strategies for Escaping Innovation Traps," *MIT Sloan Management Review*, Spring 2005, pp. 58–65.

Wong, Vanessa, "Co-Creation: Not Just Another Focus Group," *Bloomberg Businessweek* special report, April 1, 2010.

Zimmer, John, "How to Win a Marquee Account," *Sales and Marketing Management*, February 2004, p. 72.

CHAPTER 5

Decision Making: Determining Direction

Although foresight and innovation techniques provide a lot of data and insight, they are only tools. Leaders still need to make decisions. There are some similarities across all types of decisions, but there are also differences when the decision involves something as complex as a business model. As should be clear by now, a business model decision is not a discrete event that takes place at a specific point in time. It is a process that unfolds over weeks, months, or even years. This chapter describes a basic framework for decision making and then lists some of the factors most closely related to high-stakes decisions and organizational decision making.

Most people have not had formal training in decision making, and so they may seek template-driven best practices to supplant decision making. Unfortunately, templates don't necessarily teach people *how* to think. In fact, they may make it too easy to be trapped by the adequate when a better alternative may exist. Effort is required to generate alternatives beyond the obvious ones; that is why this book devotes chapters to foresight and innovation as part of the examination of business models.

THE BASIC FRAMEWORK

Let's talk a bit about the typical decision-making process. In general it involves (1) defining and framing the issue, goal, or problem requiring the decision, (2) gathering appropriate data, (3) generating alternative solutions, (4) evaluating the solutions, (5) choosing an acceptable solution, (6) acting on the chosen alternative, and (7) evaluating the outcome (see Figure 5-1).

The first step of framing the issue is not a minor point. If leaders frame a particular issue as ideas on how to return a business unit to profitability, the

FIGURE 5-1 ➤ Basic decision framework

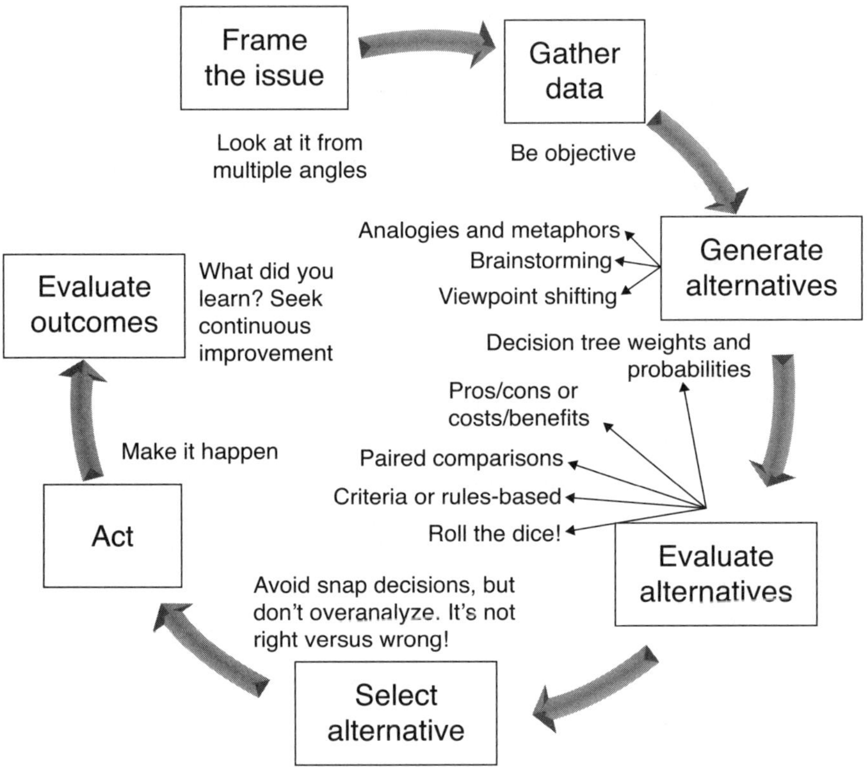

discussion probably will generate different options than will be the case if the decision is framed as ideas on how to establish ongoing value creation for the business unit.

Once the framing is done, the next two steps deal with compiling data and generating alternative solutions. Companies have used numerous tools to develop ideas, some of which may be adapted to jump-start thinking about business model redesign. For example, if you are in the insurance industry, you might use an analogy of a completely different industry: What if our insurance company had the business model of Apple? What would we do differently? Or you might ask, what if the company became part of 3M? Note that these jump-start questions started with "What if." Using what-if questions can be useful not only for generating analogies and metaphors but also to get a brainstorming session going. What if we went global? Transported a technology common in another industry to this industry? Attempted some other big-picture change? Any of these tools may be predecessors to or complements of the scenario development, integrated roadmapping, and other techniques described in Chapter 3. All are potential approaches to generating various options and alternative futures.

After generating these options, you have to evaluate them. Different approaches work in different circumstances. Sometimes listing the pros and cons of each alternative can be insight-generating and sufficient. As you go through that process, be mindful of implementation issues and possible unintended consequences. For example, if you enter a new market with different channels, what might be the consequence for your relationship with existing channel partners? Another approach to evaluating alternatives could be a simple prioritization, including weights or probabilities of outcomes. Alternatively, decision trees could be graphed for each alternative. A decision tree is a diagram of choices related to an alternative. Each choice potentially links to other choices, and the estimated outcome of each choice is defined. There also may be an opportunity to learn from the experience of other firms by collecting case examples to use for comparisons.

Sometimes the evaluation includes an analysis along predetermined criteria or rules. For example, a family-owned business may require that any business model decision maintain family ownership. Or a company may require that a business model change be consistent with its core of innovation (or efficiency or customer service). Or a company may use some variation of the balanced scorecard to evaluate the attractiveness of a particular option. These screening criteria sometimes can help a company avoid risky mistakes. Marshall & Illsley Corporation, a once-great Wisconsin bank, moved away from the conservative culture that had been its hallmark and began writing loans in volatile markets (such as Arizona) where it had no significant expertise. This was partly the result of hiring as president a former IBM executive with significant sales background who had turned Metavante Corporation into a successful data processing division but had no experience in credit. This led to a modification in the criteria for decision making with regard to loans. In 2011 the company was absorbed by its Canadian parent, Harris Bank, and as of this writing is expected to be rebranded BMO Harris Bank.

Even using these tools won't make it easy to select between two equally attractive alternatives, since either choice requires you to give up an attractive alternative. The act of carefully evaluating the issues, though, helps prepare you for the challenge of eventually selling the solution to others.

Regardless of how the alternatives are evaluated, one has to be chosen—a decision has to be made. Keep in mind that you are choosing from plausible alternatives rather than between "right" and "wrong." In many situations, making a decision work is more important than choosing the right decision. In those cases, rolling the dice may be just as appropriate as in-depth analysis. Relate the speed of the decision to the permanence of the outcome; a snap decision may be okay if the decision can be reversed easily but is risky if the decision is permanent. If the impact of the decision affects others or if others are necessary to implement the outcome, include them in the process. You need their buy-in.

In the end, decisions not only have to be made, they must be acted on. Just as carpentry tools in a tool kit will not in and of themselves build a house, decision tools will not in and of themselves provide outcomes. Leaders have to make things happen. After implementing a decision, be sure to evaluate it and teach yourself how to improve it going forward. It's worth remembering that emotion plays a role, sometimes a major role, in all decisions. Don't simply evaluate the outcome; evaluate as well the process you used to make the decision. As strategy consultant **Roch Parayre** points out, the quality of

http://www.youtube.com/watch?v=DldD9DiAyjo

a decision should be evaluated on the basis of the information you had at the time you made the decision. Was it the right decision at that time? Of course, the evaluation of process versus outcome is not an either-or examination; both must be considered. Then focus on continuous improvement for future decisions. Remember that the only way to avoid making mistakes in this process is to avoid making decisions, and that is not an option!

HIGH-STAKES DECISION MAKING

Business model decisions may be higher-stakes decisions than many of the day-to-day choices that need to be made. Therefore, it is useful to explore some additional considerations beyond the basic framework. Here are a few:

- Historical data may not be relevant.
- Many decisions are made under stress.
- Serious biases may thwart performance.
- The consequences of a wrong decision are high.
- Many people are involved in the decision.
- Business model changes trigger an ecosystem of decisions.

Historical Data May Not Be Relevant

No matter how hard we try, it's difficult to escape the status quo pull of our experience. Obviously, the more similar a new business model is to the existing (old) business model, the more relevant the historical data fit is. But the assumptions of fit must be explored. Today's and tomorrow's realities have some similarities to the past but also some differences. If we consider only the similarities, we can mislead ourselves into making the wrong decisions about the future. Unfortunately, we are likely to rationalize the decision and be unaware of the reason for the wrong choices. We have to realize that some of today's problems come from yesterday's solutions.

Staying on top of new trends and technologies helps put the past, present, and future into context. John Conover, president of Ingersoll Rand Security Technologies, points out in his end-of-chapter interview that he gathers input from numerous sources to inform his perspective on the firm's business model. He relies not only on his vice president of business development and vice president of technology and innovation but also on the 30 percent of his leadership team that is from outside North America.

Individuals should learn and practice critical thinking skills. Critical thinking refers to the process of objectively evaluating the data and assumptions surrounding an issue. Contrary to some misconceptions, critical thinking is not an effort to appraise a decision negatively with a predisposition to find flaws.

How can you develop a critical thinking competency for decision making? First, strive to be both open-minded and skeptical. (That sounds paradoxical, but both mindsets are necessary.) That means soliciting perspectives from all sides of an issue to obtain pertinent evidence before reaching a conclusion. Second, self-monitor the biases that may prevent you from being objective. Although being aware of your biases isn't enough to eliminate them, it's a start. Learn to distinguish between fact and opinion, cause and effect, selective facts and full disclosure, inquiry and advocacy. This applies to your own mental model as well as the perspectives of the people providing you with data.

However, don't completely ignore your gut reaction. Books such as *Blink* by Malcolm Gladwell, *Gut Feelings: The Intelligence of the Unconscious* by Gerd Gigerenzer, and *The Political Brain* by Drew Westen provide case studies of the role of intuition in decision making. In fact, in battle situations in which truly life-and-death decisions need to be made, hunches prove to be valuable. Just remember that your gut is an important data point but rarely the only one.

Many Decisions Are Made Under Stress

Stress can have a significant effect on your ability to make good decisions. The *New York Times* published an article highlighting some research from the journal *Science*. The researchers discovered that chronically stressed rats lost their "elastic rat cunning" and resorted to illogical rote actions such as getting food pellets they didn't eat. The researchers also discovered that the stressed animals found it difficult to revert quickly back to goal-oriented behavior. (However, after a "vacation" free of stress, the rats regained their ability to innovate and problem-solve.)

Think about the causes of the stress. Sometimes it arises from the sheer magnitude of the decision to be made, sometimes from a leader's procrastination, and sometimes from the absence of slack time in the organization. Let's consider each of these. If the major issue is the weight of the decision, try to compartmentalize it into smaller nuggets. (Of course, not all problems can be divided easily. Splitting an SUV into two pieces does not create two compact cars.) If procrastination is the root of the stress, structure the decision as a project and set realistic deadlines. If there is no slack in the organization, there will be limited ability to invest in the future. The managers, leaders, and other employees involved in making business model and strategy decisions need time to rethink processes and outcomes. Each of these stressors can diminish the efficacy of the decision-making process.

Stress can be exacerbated when you feel a deep emotional connection to the decision. Although there is almost always an emotional component to decision making, sometimes it is so significant a component that it should be dealt with head on. Just as judges recuse themselves from legal cases in which impartiality would be difficult, executives may need to take a backseat in decisions in which self-interest or emotion could impair results.

Serious Biases May Thwart Performance

Although biases are unavoidable, steps must be taken to manage or control them. That's basic common sense, right? But then, what exactly does common sense mean?

Common sense is defined as "sound practical judgment that is independent of specialized knowledge, training, or the like; normal native intelligence." We all like to think that we have it and that most business decisions are based on it. but alas, we know that's not true. Even if it were true, could we all agree on what common sense actually is? Most evidence suggests that that is not the case. Political pundits perceive their views as common sense while blasting their opponents' views as anti–common sense. Salespeople and engineers often feel the other person lacks common sense in terms of what is required to create and sell products. Individuals discover that what they perceived as common sense in their twenties may be different from what they perceive as common sense in their fifties (when their kids are twentysomethings). Short-term efforts to generate quick-fix results may derail long-term efforts focused on stable growth even though the short-term efforts are viewed as common sense.

All people bring to the table biases that result from their experiences and their functions. Biases are close cousins to rules of thumb and mindsets that serve companies and leaders well. Thus, at times these biases can have a beneficial effect by streamlining decision processes. When they are too rigid, however, they can cause leaders to hide behind some artificial notion of black and white. Therefore, it's necessary to cultivate an environment where people have the courage to challenge conventional wisdom. Otherwise companies can become stuck on former truisms or even current myths and base decisions on what is no longer true. Once myths are established without questions in a culture, they become collective beliefs.

Biases are very real and have tangible impacts on decisions. A significant bias that is reported over and over in case studies as well as quantitative research is overoptimism (or overconfidence). Both neuroscience and social science suggest that people in general are more optimistic than realistic. (Of course there is evidence that people can become collectively pessimistic while being individually optimistic.) In behavioral economics, the optimism bias is known as the positivity illusion. When executives are asked how they rate themselves on a battery of capabilities (such as driving skills) on a scale of 1 to 5, with 1 being way below average and 5 being way above average, the majority of responses are 4s or 5s, with an occasional 3. A few rare individuals will give themselves a 1 or 2. Most of us, according to Lovallo and Sibony (2006), believe we are in the top 20 percent of the population.

There is no question that optimism is necessary for risk taking. There would be no new business models, no new start-ups, and no new products without a degree of optimism. Leaders who exude confidence and are optimistic about the outcome of their planned actions generally are perceived as decisive, whereas those who carefully consider an issue from multiple angles may be viewed as indecisive. The challenge is to avoid living at either of the extreme points of this continuum. Leaders on the optimistic side should articulate how the particular decision could fail—even to the point of presuming it *will* fail—and then plan to prevent failure from happening. Indecisive managers must focus on deadlines to move forward and avoid the bias of excessive risk aversion. This can be particularly challenging when the consequences of making the wrong decision are potentially grave.

Another bias comes from assumptions and beliefs. The futurist **Patrick Dixon** uses the term *institutional blindness* to refer to the inability to be as objec-

http://www.youtube.com/watch?v=yQWMnObjunU

tive about one's own company as one is about another company. People may use assumptions and beliefs to first make decisions and later justify or rationalize the decisions with data. Be aware that people consciously or unconsciously seek facts that support what they already believe. If presented with evidence that contradicts what they believe, they have the tendency to discredit either the data or its source. If that's not possible, they remember supporting information to a greater extent than contradictory information. Although I earlier suggested that you pay attention to your intuition, try to postpone intuition as much as possible to give yourself time to evaluate your assumptions.

The Consequences of a Wrong Decision Are High

Because of the high-stakes nature of business-model change, there is a temptation to seek more and more data. As a result, managers may delay or avoid making a decision altogether. The status quo continues, and sometimes the window of opportunity shrinks or evaporates. To minimize this possibility, there are a few options to consider.

First, it's important to cultivate a culture in which failure is not equated with making the wrong decision. Recognize that uncertainty is always present in preparing for the future. Second, list various alternatives related to making the decision. Openly identify the risks of each alternative along with suggestions on how to mitigate that risk. Third, look for ways to scale back the defined problem and break it into bite-size pieces. Group those pieces into categories and rank them. These smaller elements may be more manageable. Fourth, assess the probability of both a plan A and a contingency plan B to enable a redirect if necessary. Fifth, as an extension of the prior option, attempt to rapidly test and improve on smaller projects that allow go–no-go decisions along the way. Sixth, reinforce why the status quo is not a desirable direction and support that with your rationale.

Many People Are Involved in the Decision

It's critical to involve many people to provide input into decisions of great magnitude for the firm, but the actual decision must be owned by one person or a small group of people. As hard as it may be sometimes, turn this into a positive. John Conover points out in the end-of-chapter interview the value of this: "The leadership team needs to be diverse. As the rate of change in the world continues to accelerate, an organization needs to be broad in its thinking. A leadership team with broad skills and broad life experiences brings a diversity of thought that provides the depth of thought required today."

Arriving at consensus without succumbing to groupthink can be a challenge. However, there are some steps that can help:

- Make sure the right people are involved for this particular decision. Determine the appropriate level of involvement; some will be deciders, and others will be subject matter experts who provide input into the decision.
- Assign homework before meetings. Assemble people's insights before discussing conclusions to underscore assumptions and biases.
- Manage the process. Establish appropriate ground rules for the meetings. Encourage open discussion and recognize valid disagreements. Force people to consider opposing views. Have individuals write down their conclusions before arriving at a group decision. Stop debate after the decision has been reached.

Business Model Changes Trigger an Ecosystem of Decisions

"Everything changes everything." That's what was stated on a sign in the darkroom of a photography class I took years ago. Change the exposure by a couple of seconds, change the f-stop a notch, change the strength of the chemicals—any and all of these things affect the final picture. That may be obvious in a situation in which the physical and chemical reactions represent something of an ecosystem. What about decisions in business, education, and government? You're still dealing with ecosystems, but the interrelationships are somewhat looser and consequently may be overlooked.

We live in a world where so many trends are happening simultaneously that people begin to feel overwhelmed when they try to apply trend insights to decision making. Should we be specialists in a limited number of trend areas or generalists across many? Since both are necessary (and almost mutually exclusive), generalists need to be synthesizers of the knowledge obtained through specialists. For example, molecular biology is a very specialized discipline in which progress is made by describing small bits, usually one at a time, such as one strand of protein or one strand of RNA. Specialization is important in fully understanding these individual bits of knowledge. However, these bits of knowledge don't always help one understand the complete organism of which they are a part.

Scientists increasingly are applying these components of knowledge to a systems understanding of organisms, including the interacting network of genes, proteins, and chemical reactions.

Let's look at another example of ecosystem impacts: products designed to reduce crop damage through the use of pesticides to kill insects. The overall goal of the product—the intended benefit to customers—is to improve the crop yield. However, if the entire emphasis is on chemicals to eliminate the insects, there may be an unintended consequence of insects becoming resistant to the pesticide. (Similar concerns have been raised with respect to the overuse of antibiotics.) A systems perspective broadens the viewpoint beyond the chemical composition of the insecticide to the higher goal of reducing crop damage.

Similarly, business model decisions should not be made in a vacuum. Understanding the context is critical. Systems thinking is the foundation of comprehensive decision making. Although many managers work to resolve short-term problems by focusing on the individual pieces, they also should be open to the way in which that particular thing interacts with other factors on a higher level. In fact, the systems approach may result in strikingly different conclusions than would be the case with singular analyses.

We've all heard the phrase "you can't see the forest for the trees," meaning that we can get so caught up with the day-to-day events that we are unable to see (or we overlook) the big picture. I suspect we've all been guilty of that to some degree. However, one of my clients made this axiom even stronger when he said his company's managers can't see the forest *or* the trees because they're too busy eating the dirt! That's really getting enshrouded with minutia.

Many systems thinking courses use some variation of the beer game, in which different participants take on the role of manufacturer, wholesaler, or retailer. Each tries to achieve a balance between too much and too little inventory in their own businesses even though the consequence may be supply chain imbalances.

A systems framework expands the context for strategies and business models. Competition continues to morph, and strategies should reflect those changes. Google saw explosive growth as a search engine for everything, but as is often the case with market leaders, competitors begin to nibble around the edges. Individuals interested in purchasing products now may start at Amazon, and others interested in people and events may start at Facebook. The shifting competitive landscape provides a different context for strategy development.

Similarly, the strategies in the mobile market have shifted, according to experts, from a battle of devices to a war of ecosystems. Since all cell phones can talk to one another and connect to the same websites and e-mail systems, it's not just product strategy but network (or platform) strategy that needs to be part of the business models of companies in this industry.

ORGANIZATIONAL DECISION MAKING

Decisions can be made by individuals and by groups, as was suggested in the prior two sections, but they also can be influenced by the organizations of which they are a part. Thus, there are three levels or hubs of decision making (see Figure 5-2). There are both formal and informal decision networks at work here. The formal network specifies who has the authority to make decisions at a particular risk, financial, or strategic impact level. It helps prioritize and allocate decisions to the appropriate individual, department, or team, and it suggests the protocol and procedures required to maintain stability while minimizing risk.

The formal organizational network should be examined periodically to determine whether it is relevant for a new business model. In fact, some companies have put together multifunctional teams to design more effective decision-making processes. They start by tracing various decisions through

FIGURE 5-2 ➤ Decision hubs

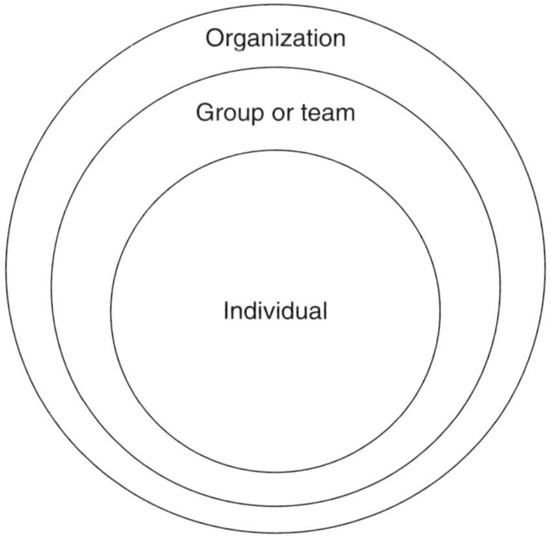

the organization, defining inputs, outputs, and results. This would include a description of decision rights (who has authority), identification of unnecessary approvals or bottlenecks in light of the priority of the decision, and a determination of whether decision rights should be allocated to different individuals (or teams or departments). Decisions categorized as routine, for example, might have a different process than those for truly transformative decisions.

Thomas Davenport (2009) suggested a four-step approach to improving the organizational decision making process:

1. Identify and prioritize decisions. Select the top decisions related to your strategy or business model renewal and place the greatest emphasis on those decisions.
2. Assess the factors required to make the decision. Think about how and how well this type of decision has been made historically in your company and how to improve the process. Develop an inventory of models that may be relevant to related types of decisions in the company.
3. Define roles, processes, and systems. Describe the behaviors you believe will make decision making more effective. Consider qualitative and quantitative factors that may have different value for different decisions.
4. Institutionalize the new approach. Teach managers how to decide how to decide. Provide tools and training so that they are more apt to determine when a decision can be made unilaterally, when a vote is preferred, who should be accountable for results, and who should be informed.

Davenport described how Chevron established a decision-analysis group to facilitate workshops, help managers create models and interpret results, and assess decision quality. The company regularly performs "lookbacks" on decisions to judge both the process and the outcomes. Recalibration is always a good idea. There are many, many tools business professionals can use to make decisions. None of them are perfect, but most have value. It's sometimes a matter of putting a stick in the ground and acting on it.

How does that relate to business model renewal? With competitive and external pressures to create more dynamic organizations, companies are beginning to establish business model portfolios that require moving decision-making authority closer to the front lines. That's going to demand an upskilling of decision-making knowledge at all levels as well as a change in the authority for making decisions. This doesn't mean that everyone will become a strategist. Rather, individuals must know how to make day-to-day decisions that don't derail current efforts to move from the status quo toward desired futures. That means senior leaders must move from managing activities to developing people even if the consequences are chaotic at times.

JOHN CONOVER

DECISION MAKING IS A CRITICAL PART OF LEADERSHIP

John W. Conover IV was named senior vice president and president of Ingersoll Rand's Security Technologies Sector in July 2009. John brings over 30 years of knowledge and experience working in the commercial building marketplace. Most recently, he served as president of Trane Commercial Systems, Americas, where he successfully drove the business's evolution from being primarily an equipment provider to becoming an integrated systems, services, and controls business. Prior positions include vice president, district manager, sales leader, and sales engineer. John currently leads Ingersoll Rand's sustainability strategy council. He holds a bachelor's degree in civil engineering from Lehigh University.

John W. Conover IV
President
Ingersoll Rand, Security Technologies

John, you've seen tremendous changes since joining Trane in 1977 as a sales engineer and eventually becoming president of Ingersoll Rand's Security Technologies Sector. Can you talk a bit about the dramatic business shifts you experienced in those thirty-plus years?

One of the largest transformations I've seen, and was proud to be a part of, is when Trane embraced a new mindset about how it interacts with customers. They realized that greater customer intimacy could be realized when they stopped being an equipment seller—which was strictly transactional—and became a solutions partner. For example, Morgan Stanley called one day and said, "We need some HVAC equipment." Under their new operating model, Trane didn't just show up with a catalog. Their response was more in line with today's version of *CSI*, the TV show. We asked questions that weren't expected: What were all of the activities that happened in the building? Was Morgan Stanley interested in green solutions? Were they worried about power failures? Trane taught its engineers and sales force that more inquiry, and less talking, helps us get beneath the surface of a customer's HVAC needs to better address that customer's fundamental business concerns. That mindset shift was a huge game changer for Trane, in the United States and globally as well. At Ingersoll Rand, we're also similarly focusing on solutions more than ever.

When you are dealing with major developments like this, how do you prepare yourself to make decisions?

I make sure I'm listening to feedback from inside *and* outside my business to confirm I'm not enamored of my own great idea. Leaders must seek out feedback from those with different opinions and experiences. When planning a project, initiative, or investment, you have to ensure you aren't insulated. If you're surrounded by yes men and women all the time, I believe your failures will be greater than your successes. Also, decisions should be data-driven to the extent feasible to make certain that decisions are as intelligent and informed as possible, with the realization that risk will always be present. In the end you need to take the input, make a decision, and act. As leaders, we need to have a bias for action.

You are credited with playing an important role in driving the evolution of Trane's Americas business from being primarily an equipment business to becoming an integrated systems, services, and controls business. What were some of the steps involved in the transformation?

This shift in culture doesn't happen just because management sends out a memo. Employees have to embrace the change to a solutions business. You need to communicate relentlessly to your folks in the field, make sure that they know where you are going and that they share the vision of being a bold new company. We also aligned organizational structure, compensation, and recognition with the new direction of the business.

So it sounds as if you view employees as critical to strategy execution. How do you ensure clarity of vision—and the appropriate talent—to avoid a breakdown between strategy and execution?

This is a classic change management process. As stated above, communicate relentlessly to help ensure your workforce is aligned and working on the right things. Celebrate the early wins. Get your leadership to visit sites to have this validated for themselves in skip-level meetings. Ask what's working. What does our vision mean to you? What's in the way of you doing your job and serving the customer? It's important that leadership remains visible in the process.

Employees want to meet their leaders, and they crave interaction. We use some simple tools to ensure that our frontline leaders also are sharing the right messages—consistent messages—with our employees. Even a simple key messages of the month mailing helps cascade results, priorities, and behaviors to your workforce. At the end of the day, I'm not the most important person that impacts employee engagement. It's an employee's direct boss who has the most critical communications and engagement role in the organization.

Beyond efforts to share a common vision, how do you empower employees to make decisions for their particular piece of the business?

First and foremost, you have to trust them to do their job. Hiring excellent people, investing in their development, aligning on the vision, and clearly understanding the boundaries are the keys to success. Let your employees make the decision within those boundaries. They are closer to the action and to the customer than I am. Empowered employees are more satisfied, develop faster, and create a learning organization culture. In a learning organization, we create a safe environment where contrarian views are encouraged and even some failures—driven by the right motivators—are celebrated. There is a clear correlation between employee engagement, customer satisfaction, and corporate profitability.

Ingersoll Rand's CEO, Mike Lamach, has announced the company is betting on growth from innovation and emerging markets. How do you stay on top of new trends and technologies to help pursue this vision?

I have two key roles on my senior leadership team that help keep me in touch with business trends and innovation to share interesting breakthroughs, ideas, and industry buzz. I rely heavily on my VP of business development as well as my VP of technology and innovation. Also, as we look at emerging markets, 30 percent of my leadership team is from outside North America. But interaction, along with getting out of the office, is also key. You have to interact with customers in their offices or at their projects. You have to interact at key industry trade shows. I also stay connected with thought leaders in our business.

Sustainability is an important focus of many corporations. Tell us about your efforts as the leader of IR's sustainability strategy council.

I'm excited to share that Ingersoll Rand just completed a global survey as a partner with *The Economist* magazine on the perception gap between CEOs and their senior leaders. We found that the C-suite execs are misaligned with the next few layers down regarding the importance of sustainability and energy efficiency initiatives in their own companies.

We had 278 survey participants and found that respondents beneath the C-suite are significantly more likely (61 percent versus

49 percent) to say that their organizations do not do enough to integrate energy efficiency initiatives into business strategy. This is critical as funding, implementation, and prioritization require executive-level support. Lack of support can mean lack of progress.

We also found that companies find it difficult to assess their energy use and then make progress in reducing it. Only 26 percent of survey respondents said their organization has conducted an energy audit, and around 22 percent said they do no measurement at all.

We also uncovered an interesting gap within these companies—the supply chain is too often overlooked in looking at energy efficiency initiatives and opportunities. For many companies, particularly retailers and those who outsource their manufacturing, total energy consumption occurs mostly in the supply chain. Yet most organizations tend to focus internally, with few looking outside their direct operations to their supply chain. Just 8 percent said energy efficiency was a priority for suppliers, and only 4 percent said they had worked with suppliers in this area.

At the end of the day, we found that investing in energy efficiency programs turns out to be a great bet for executives looking for paybacks that are fast, may deliver up to a seven-to-one return on investment, and engage employees at the same time.

Do you have any words of wisdom for executives struggling with refining their business models as they move into the future?

Three thoughts drive my decisions today:

First, now more than ever we need to stay focused on the customer. By watching our customers and understanding their issues and preferences, we can create solutions for their unmet needs.

Second, the organization needs to stay nimble. Invert the corporate pyramid and put the customer on top. Quickly and efficiently bringing those solutions to market will create sustainable advantage.

Third, the leadership team needs to be diverse. As the rate of change in the world continues to accelerate, an organization needs to be broad in its thinking. A leadership team with broad skills and broad life experiences brings the diversity of thought that provides the depth of thought required today.

REFERENCES

Angier, Natalie, "Brain Is a Co-Conspirator in a Vicious Stress Loop," *New York Times*, August 18, 2009, p. D2.

Ariely, Dan, "The Curious Paradox of Optimism Bias," *BusinessWeek*, August 24 and 31, 2009, p. 48.

Arnst, Catherine, "Why Snap Decisions Work," *BusinessWeek*, August 20 and 27, 2007, p. 110.

Burrows, Pete, "Mobile Wars!" *Bloomberg Businessweek*, February 21–27, 2011, pp. 37–39.

Carey, Benedict, "In Battle, Hunches Prove to be Valuable," *New York Times*, July 28, 2009, p. A1.

Cross, Rob, Robert J. Thomas, and David A. Light, "How 'Who You Know' Affects What You Decide," *MIT Sloan Management Review*, Winter 2009, pp. 35–42.

Davenport, Thomas, "Make Better Decisions," *Harvard Business Review*, November 2009, pp. 117–123.

Finkelstein, Sydney, Jo Whitehead, and Andrew Campbell, "The Illusion of Smart Decision Making: The Past Is Not Prologue," *Journal of Business Strategy*, 2009, issue 6, p. 36.

Lovallo, Dan, and Olivier Sibony, "The Case for Behavioral Strategy," *McKinsey Quarterly*, March 2010.

Lovallo, Dan, and Olivier Sibony, "Distortions and Deceptions in Strategic Decisions," *McKinsey Quarterly*, January 2006.

Lovallo, Dan, and Olivier Sibony, "Taking the Bias out of Meetings," *McKinsey Quarterly*, March 2010.

Sharot, Tali, "The Optimism Bias," *Time*, June 6, 2011, pp. 41–46.

Sorrell, Sir Martin, Randy Komisar, and Anne Mulcahy, "How We Do It: Three Executives Reflect on Strategic Decision Making," *McKinsey Quarterly*, March 2010.

Spivak, Cary, "M&I's Dead End," JSOnline, July 9, 2011.

PART 3

Business Models: Aligning to Make Things Happen

This section moves from exploration to action: making things happen. Chapter 6 defines the role of a contextual leader in determining the relevant tone for sustaining, transformative, and disruptive growth strategies and business models. Chapter 7 highlights the importance of connecting long- and short-term plans. Chapter 8 explores the challenges of managing change and aligning organizational culture.

CHAPTER 6

Contextual Leadership

Leadership has been examined and poked and prodded from every angle but remains an elusive concept. There have been many comparisons and contrasts between leadership and management.

John Kotter (1990) has stated:

> *Leadership and management are two distinctive and complementary systems of action. Management is about coping with complexity. Leadership is about coping with change. Leadership complements management; it doesn't replace it. Companies manage complexity by planning and budgeting, by controlling and problem solving. By contrast, leading an organization begins by setting direction, aligning people to the direction, and inspiring people to achieve a vision.*

To restate, management is about coping with complexity whereas leadership is about coping with change. Managers are expected to deliver predictable results as promised; leaders are expected to generate changes and breakthroughs. Managers capitalize on skillful utilization of resources to reach a visible goal. They typically are concerned with day-to-day how-to-get-it-done issues. Leaders guide and direct a course of action into a changing future, usually by influencing others. They must motivate and inspire others, often in challenging conditions. There are times when it is most important to a decision (leadership) and other times when it is more important to make a decision work (management). In reality, there is a very blurred line between leadership and management, and improving on both skills can help strategy and business model renewal efforts.

According to Warren Bennis (1994), all leaders seem to have some common traits. The first is a guiding vision or purpose. You must have a clear idea of your personal and professional goals and a willingness to pursue them.

A second characteristic is passion along with the ability to infuse that passion into others. A third characteristic is integrity, a combination of self-knowledge, candor, and maturity. Curiosity, the thirst for knowledge, is the fourth characteristic. Fifth, a leader has to be daring and take risks. Bennis goes on to say: "The most dangerous myth is that leaders are born—that there is a genetic factor to leadership, that people have certain charismatic qualities or not. That's nonsense. Leaders are made rather than born."

Of course, there are some inborn traits that are helpful. Truly gifted leaders seem to have an innate ability to select and motivate people; this is a skill that can be improved but not created from scratch. Leaders also seem to have a flair for good judgment to a greater extent than most people. Just as in any other debate over nature versus nurture, leadership evolves from some complicated interconnections between genetic predispositions and life and business experiences.

THE ROLE OF THE INDIVIDUAL IN LEADERSHIP

The role of individual figureheads in leading a company through turbulence is hotly debated. Examples abound of founders returning to leadership positions when businesses begin to falter. Steve Jobs is perhaps a classic example. After losing a power struggle with the board in 1984, he left Apple and started NeXT. Apple bought NeXT in 1996, and Jobs returned as CEO in 1997. His impact on the trajectory of the company cannot be denied. It will be insightful to watch changes in corporate culture and strategy following his death in 2011.

Michael Dell founded Dell in 1984 and served as CEO until 2004. Although he didn't leave the company, he turned over the leadership reins to Kevin Rollins. Competitive pressures increased during Rollins's tenure, and the company began to show signs of decline. Michael Dell returned to the position of CEO in 2007 and began to evolve the firm beyond its core PC products.

Howard Schultz joined Starbucks as director of operations and marketing in 1982, when the company sold only whole-bean and ground coffee—no beverages. Schultz left the original Starbucks, opened two espresso bars, then came back and merged the two companies in 1987. There was dramatic growth during the next decade. During the 2000s (Schultz stepped down as CEO in 2000), growth spiraled out of control, and the company began to lose its soul. Schultz came back to the position of CEO in 2008 with a goal of transforming the company by returning to its core values. In fall 2010, Starbucks posted its best financial position in its nearly 40-year history.

The role of the founder leader was important in these three companies. What about companies that continue to exist long after their founders?

Is the role of leadership as identifiable and singular? This is where it's less clear-cut. When George Fisher took over Motorola in the 1980s, he was credited with a remarkable transformation of the company. He was recruited in 1993 by Kodak to provide a similar turnaround; it was believed at the time that only an outsider (the first in Kodak's history) could bring about the radical transformation necessary to save the company, which was stalled in its evolution from film to digital photography. However, circumstances in the Kodak environment and culture were substantially different from what existed for Fisher at Motorola, and the company continued to face challenges. When Fisher left in 1999, he was replaced by Daniel Carp, a lifelong Kodak employee.

There are other examples of mixed results when leaders were hired to transform a company, presumably by applying the same skills that worked for them in a prior firm. When Robert Nardelli became Home Depot's CEO in 2001, he brought with him the GE culture but not experience with the strategy and culture of a retailing operation such as Home Depot. He left at the end of 2006. Similarly, James McNerney brought GE's Six Sigma philosophy to 3M during his 2001–2005 tenure as CEO but was perceived not to have the DNA for innovation that was core to 3M's culture. It seems that leadership is most effective when it fits the current context of the organization and its environment.

LEADERSHIP AND FOLLOWERSHIP

Leadership implies followership, and followership depends partly on culture and context. In some sense, leadership is defined by followership, and leaders without followers cannot engender change. Most experts agree that there is no single leadership style that is appropriate for all situations. It's not a science that can be boiled down to four or five characteristics. It's personal and at times defies generalization. Nevertheless, leadership concepts can be learned and developed, though the result has to be authentic and contextually relevant for it to work. The context is derived from the mission, structure, culture, and values of the organization; knowledge of external factors uncovered in the environmental scan; the vision and plausible futures derived through foresight and innovation efforts; attention to the resource requirements; and the degree of change compared with the status quo. Of course, that's easier said than done.

Rare is the business leader who is both a visionary (who can sense the future) and an actionary (who can manage the present) regardless of the business context. The agility to adopt the appropriate stance without losing authenticity is a true challenge and comes from experience. Many organizations encourage employees to work in different business units and divisions to gain skills in diverse environments and cultures. This may include promotions but also lateral moves and occasionally downward moves. The risk and the willingness to change are an important part of the learning process. Contextual leaders also tend to be well read, with involvement on boards and groups external to the company. Then in 2012 Eastman Kodak filed for bankruptcy.

Recruiters recognize that leadership prospects who have experience in limited contextual diversity are less likely to be successful in leading major transformations. They also observe that executives groomed in a very strong culture may have a difficult time transitioning to another culture. In a 2009 *BusinessWeek* interview, several recruiters indicated they were hesitant to recruit from a couple of noted technical companies because of their "testosterone-driven, take-no-prisoners" cultures. Of course, it would depend on the type of company they were recruiting for.

Even company founders brought back to run their companies a second time have to go beyond the status quo. As Starbucks's Howard Schultz said in *Onward*, "effective second-time CEOs recognize that what they built the first time was not a religion. They accept that change is inevitable."

Leadership requires agility and contextual intelligence. Effective leaders have to judge from the context of the situation whether an autocratic decision is required or whether it's the opposite. They have to adjust their style to fit the circumstances and the needs of the followers. There are times when inspiration is most critical and other times when the transactional skills of motivating employees to implement a strategy—making them more productive—becomes more important.

In an interesting May 2011 *Harvard Business Review* interview with David Allen (author of *Getting Things Done*) and Tony Schwartz (author of *Be Excellent at Anything*), the consultants were asked: "What role do leaders play in making workers more productive?" The question dealt with the more transactional aspects of a leader's job. Here are their answers:

> *Schwartz: The leader's role is to be the chief energy officer. It's to mobilize and focus and direct and inspire and regularly recharge those he or she leads.*
>
> *Allen: If bosses don't appropriately manage the tasks for which people are coming to work, it's impossible for employees to get the bandwidth to do what Tony is talking about. If jobs are not clear, if projects are not well defined, if outcomes are not focused on, if action steps and accountabilities and responsibilities are not allocated, then the leader hasn't done his job.*

All these examples are part of the contextual intelligence required for agile leadership. But there's more. Contextual leadership also requires emotional intelligence: the ability to deal with one's own and others' emotions. The concept of emotional intelligence (EI) has been around for decades, and its validity has been questioned. Widely different methods and measurement approaches have been used to study it, and the bulk of EI research has focused on transformational leadership, mostly in Western countries. Nevertheless, even with those concerns, empirical evidence seems to support EI's relevance for leadership.

Emotional Intelligence

EI (also referred to as EQ) is commonly associated with the work of **Daniel Goleman** an author, psychologist, and former science journalist, in his 1996

http://www.youtube.com/watch?v=7QvOo1oh9f4&feature=player_embedded#!

book *Emotional Intelligence: Why It Can Matter More Than IQ*. The tenth anniversary edition came out in 2006. *Emotional Intelligence 2.0* by Travis Bradberry and Jean Greaves is a 2009 entry into the field. Goleman initially listed five domains of emotional intelligence (and eventually reduced it to four), whereas Bradberry and Greaves list four, but the philosophy of EI is similar not just between these two sources but compared with other perspectives on emotional intelligence.

For simplicity this chapter will focus on Goleman's original five dimensions (self-awareness, self-management, motivation, empathy, and social skills) and relate them to effective leadership (Figure 6-1):

1. Self-awareness refers to a leader's ability to be cognizant of and honest about his or her emotions, strengths, weaknesses, drives, and values. If you know your personal values, you are less likely to make decisions that go against them and could cause inner turmoil. It requires knowledge of your capabilities so that when making strategic decisions you don't set yourself up for failure. When you feel an emotion, practice pausing to allow yourself time to understand it.
2. Self-management refers to a leader's ability to control his or her temper, maintain composure, and keep his or her emotions in check.

FIGURE 6-1 ➤ Emotional intelligence

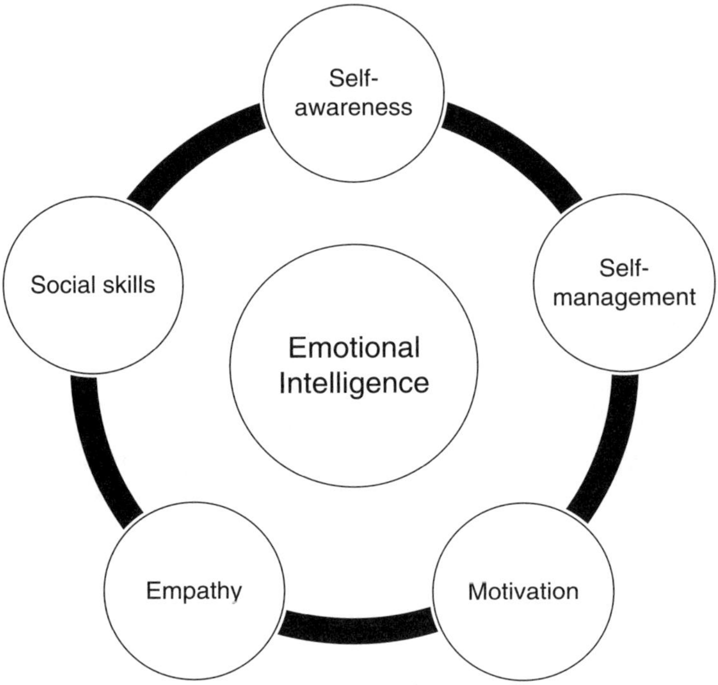

It also implies being conscientious and taking responsibility for one's actions to build trust and integrity. When you feel a disruptive emotion, stop and ask yourself why you're feeling this way and how you can redirect the emotion in a positive way. Recognize your own assumptions and reframe situations to get a broader perspective.

3. Motivation refers to a leader's ability to enter into an emotional state associated with a drive to succeed. It involves guiding or facilitating progress toward a goal, including initiative to act on opportunities, alignment of individual and organizational goals, and optimism about the process. To build motivation, have a personal vision and recognize (i.e., psychologically reward yourself for) small successes that move you toward that vision. Do the same thing for others.
4. Empathy refers to a leader's ability to treat others according to their emotional reactions. This is not sympathy but a thoughtful consideration of others' feelings. It means sensing the perspectives and development needs of others. The challenge with empathy is

that when you try to put yourself in someone else's shoes, you may think that persons feel the way you would in that situation. That may or may not be true. Listen to tone of voice and observe facial expressions and other cues people may be giving you and add those observations to your efforts to understand.

5. The dimension of social skills refers to a leader's ability to build and mend relationships, to engage productively with all stakeholders and work collaboratively toward a shared goal. It includes the ability to influence others by using effective diplomacy, listen openly, and create inspiration. Sometimes the hard part about building relations is starting them; asking questions and telling stories can establish this foundation. Nevertheless, follow-through will be necessary for lasting trust and confidence.

TRANSFORMATIONAL LEADERSHIP

Transformational leadership is a particular style of leadership that generally is identified with efforts to change individuals and social systems. It often is contrasted with other styles, such as charismatic, transactional, and servant leadership. Smith, Montagno, and Kuzmenko (2004), for example, examined the contextual factors for which a transformational style as opposed to a servant leadership style might be more appropriate. They suggested that servant leaders, who often arise within cultures of egalitarianism, have a tendency to be connected to a "spiritual generative culture." Transformational leaders, in contrast, are motivated by a sense of mission to survive in a challenging environment; this is more likely to spawn an "empowered dynamic culture." Servant leaders are more apt to focus on the personal growth of followers, whereas transformational leaders focus on change and development of the organization itself.

The authors further postulated that servant leadership is more appropriate in static environments (often with relatively low complexity) and that transformational leadership is more appropriate in dynamic environments where risk taking and innovation become increasingly important. The greater the uncertainty and turbulence in an environment are, the more likely it is that a leader will need transformational skills. On the basis of that logic, I am proposing that executives leading efforts to reinvent a business model—moving beyond being a status quo defender or incremental improver—will lean toward the skills of a transformational leader. These skills, as shown in Figure 6-2, include (1) understanding the need for organizational changes,

FIGURE 6-2 ➤ Transformational leadership

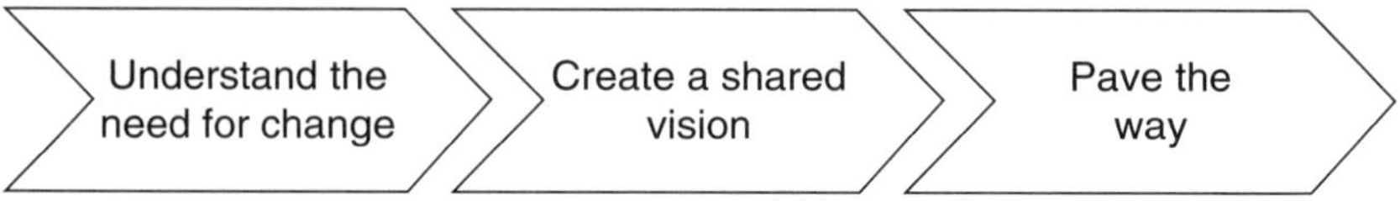

(2) creating and inspirationally communicating a shared vision of what the organization can be, and (3) paving the way to make that vision a reality.

Understanding the Need for Change

Researching and examining the need for organizational change has been covered in the earlier chapters of this book, so I have just a few additional comments to make here. Although it's important to understand the need for change, it's also important for leaders to consider the balance of short-term stability and long-term viability of the organization. Rowe and Nejad (2009) suggest that strategic leaders who balance the conflicting pull of managerial and visionary demands envision the future with the present-day circumstances in mind. Thus, they must formulate strategies both for immediate impact and for preservation of long-term goals to enhance organizational survival.

Savage and Sales (2008) suggest that in a turbulent business environment, what is necessary is an anticipatory leader who embodies the traits of futurist, strategist, and integrator. The futurist trait requires a relentless devotion to understanding trends, sensing the future, and discerning patterns that may affect the organization. As a strategist, an anticipatory leader looks for possibilities the trends portend, for plausible futures and insights from a systems perspective. Integration requires bringing everything and everyone together and introducing the tactical steps that drive day-to-day activities. Ground the integration in ways that test your assumptions and provide metrics to gauge progress. Think through an honest assessment of the capability to drive the transformation process. No sacred cows can be allowed to graze undisturbed. This is where a shared vision becomes critical.

Creating a Shared Vision

Although creating a shared vision might seem within the realm of a servant leader, it's also important for a transformational leader. A shared vision is the product of many visions and many imaginations, and there is no best-practice template for a vision statement. A vision statement is an aspirational and inspirational description of an organization's future.

Think about the term *vision.* At a basic level, a vision is an image, often connected with an ability to foresee the future. So it is with a strategic vision; it is a vivid image of the future, a depiction of what the organization will look like at a future point in time. It helps stakeholders envision future opportunities and begin to visualize a road map going forward

Vision statements should be more than altruistic platitudes. They should paint a picture of the products, services, customers, and/or technologies that will be in the company's future, along with an indication of how the company will thrive or compete in that environment. The length of a vision statement is less critical than its impact. President Kennedy's aspiration for the United States to put a man on the moon by 1969 was essentially a vision statement. Highly complex and sophisticated plans and activities were required to fulfill it, but the end point was clear.

A vision statement sometimes is likened to a future annual report. If you wrote an annual report for five years from now, what would it say? Where and how would you be competing? How and why would you be winning? What goals would you have accomplished? And why should the rest of the company care? Remember that an unrealistic vision isn't vision—it's hallucination.

Let's use a scene from the movie *Other People's Money* (1991) to contrast the effectiveness of two vision statements. The basic plot involves New England Wire & Cable, a hypothetical industrial firm, facing a hostile takeover by corporate raider Lawrence Garfield, aka Larry the Liquidator, played by Danny DeVito. The firm has seen better days but is not debt-ridden. The patriarch of the company, Andrew Jorgenson (played by Gregory Peck), wants to stay in the wire and cable business even though Garfield is intent on liquidation. Each presents his visio" at the company's shareholders' meeting, after which the stockholders cast their decisive votes. The YouTube speeches are hyperlinked in the next paragraph. If possible, listen to the two speeches before reading further.)

The meeting begins with **Gregory Peck** sharing his appeal to the

http://www.youtube.com/watch?v=Uundu-aPiBQ

shareholders to continue supporting the business as it exists. After he finishes, **Danny DeVito** provides his rebuttal and rationale for liquidation.

http://www.youtube.com/watch?v=MfL7STmWZ1c

Think about the tone and content of the two speeches. Gregory Peck embodies the servant leader, honest and caring about the employees. Danny DeVito has a less conciliatory tone but also provides a more concrete road map to the future. They both maintain their authenticity, but DeVito establishes a more visible shared vision, especially since the audience consists of stockholders. Although this is a hypothetical example, it's a good reminder of the essential components of communicating a vision statement. A transformational leader clearly and forcefully communicates and dramatizes the vision for change.

Paving the Way

Inspiring followers to pursue a vision is not the end. Transformational leaders have to work to ensure that the structure and resources are appropriate and available. They need to define the tools and resources required to mobilize and sustain organizational change initiatives (see Chapter 8).

Redesign the organization as necessary to support the transformation. Ensure that the structure and infrastructure reinforce the new vision and strategic direction. Identify the sources of future capital that may be required. Determine whether the culture enhances or inhibits movement along the new critical path. Define the competencies necessary to move forward; devise plans and reallocate resources to develop the competencies. Implement a robust process of education. Establish listening posts to receive timely feedback. Remove barriers to success.

Obviously, business model transformation cannot be accomplished by one person. Just as it takes a community to raise a child, it takes a team to renew a firm. Think through the role that leaders at all levels will play in the change.

Building Leaders at All Levels

For large-scale change to happen in an organization, there have to be leaders at multiple levels. Notice that I used the word *leader* (not *implementer*) here. Managers and others who become change agents want to be able to lead rather than simply follow orders. That means that leaders at higher levels must empower their managers to lead and make some independent decisions rather than just try to force implementation through them. Thus, leadership development becomes an important part of the overall process.

Many executives feel that leadership development is a job for the human resources (HR) department, with an emphasis on generic skills. But if companies are serious about establishing a portfolio of business models, there will have to be contextual leaders with the bench strength to make that possible. That requires an outline of required competencies at multiple levels. Create the environment for leaders to develop more competencies through formal and informal techniques, including shuffling high-potential managers throughout the company as appropriate to gain the requisite skills.

LEADERSHIP ESSENTIALS: EXPERT ADVICE COLUMN BY GUEST CONTRIBUTOR SCOTT LINGREN, DIRECTOR OF CORPORATE STRATEGY AND BUSINESS TRANSFORMATION FOR FREESCALE SEMICONDUCTOR

Aside from the specific things that leaders must do to implement a strategy, my experience has been that there are three factors that transcend any specific project or time frame and will closely correlate to success both personally and professionally. These are passion, focus, and ownership.

Passion

This is all about that positive energy that naturally burns in all of us for those things most dear to us and true to our nature. It is the drive that makes us feel alive, that brings joy and a sense of fulfillment and purpose, and that for many us defines who we are.

We all meet people we instantly know have passion for who they are and what they do. I believe it is that infectious energy in passionate people that generates most of the world's great achievements, big and small. Some make the headlines of newspapers or win awards, and others produce small daily flashes of greatness that make this world a better place. As a manager, I would strongly encourage you to hire only those people who you sense have a passion for the position you are filling, or at least for your team or company charter. Uncoachable traits such as passion are invaluable to building a strong, supportive, largely self-guided team.

We spend a considerable amount of time at our places of employment. For many of us, it's nearly as much—or perhaps more—awake time as we spend outside of work. In many ways this seems crazy (and probably is), but if that's the course you choose, you should certainly get some joy out of it. So find something you want to do, where you feel you are making a difference. That doesn't have to be curing cancer or feeding the poor, but it does have to make you happy and give you a sense of purpose and fulfillment.

Wake up in the morning and be enthusiastic about your life and your place in it! It doesn't all have to be perfect (which is good because it never is), but this is your life, so no one else is going to invest in you if you don't. I know this is a platitude at best, but it's true. You only go around once.

Focus

There are a great many who have said that trying to please everyone means guaranteeing that you please no one. Or that trying to accomplish everything —or even just too many things—means nothing gets done right. Focusing is an exceptionally difficult skill; that is why so few people are good at it. Even in the best of circumstances, where schedules are reasonable, resources are available, and fire drills come in at a manageable pace, focus and prioritization can be tough. (Can you even remember a time as ideal as that?)

Layer in the realities of today's overstretched workloads and you quickly find that trying to do it all virtually ensures failure. More teams are now doing the work of 10 with a staff of 3, have budgets that are fractions of what they were a few years ago, or need to accomplish many of the same tasks in half the previous time. It will make us all crazy if we let it.

Choosing what to focus on is so challenging, I believe, because in many ways it forces us to choose what not to focus on. Pushing projects to a lower priority is surprisingly painful at times, especially projects are urgent, are fun to do, or feel like they should be top priority. But without some prioritization, you may be crushed under the weight of all those top priorities.

So what can a manager do to better manage her time and workload and provide some guidance and suggestions to her team? The first is to understand what I call "the tyranny of the urgent" and the other is to understand "juggling glass."

The Tyranny of the Urgent

We are living in a world that is increasingly addicted to the immediate.

Maybe it started in our personal lives with TV dinners in the 1970s or the rise of fast food in the 1980s. But in our work lives I would maintain that it accelerated greatly with the mass adoption of personal computers and the explosion of cellular telephones in the late 1980s and early 1990s. Suddenly information was flying around much faster than ever before, and the expectation began to form that you could reach virtually anyone in a short amount of time. E-mail began to emerge. Presentations and contracts could be created by individuals instead of the administrative department. Leaving the office did not mean you were disconnected from the business information world—at least not completely. We were beginning to be truly connected, and when the Internet moved from being a niche information access system for universities to being a mainstream information source, the transition to centralized information sources and real-time connectivity was complete.

Not so many years later we had lost the ability to manage our own time, to set priorities, to focus. Our work world is dominated by last-minute requests, fire drills, drop-ins, and requests that "will only take a minute." We can be yanked around like puppets if we let it all dictate our lives. This is what I call the tyranny of the urgent. So stop taking every phone call or checking every e-mail the moment it arrives and power off your BlackBerry when you get home. Decide to take back your life today.

Juggling Glass

We all know the tired but often accurate metaphor of juggling balls to represent the attempted management of our many projects and time demands. Picturing all those balls in the air is a good way of visualizing our roles as jugglers, keeping as many in the air as possible.

What we should stop to think about is that these balls may look quite similar, but upon careful inspection it is revealed that they are not all made the same. Actually, some of the balls are made of rubber and some are made of glass. The glass balls are the ones that are the most important, the most closely tied to our success and happiness, the ones we absolutely, positively must not drop. No matter what, these balls stay in the air and take top priority. The other balls are made of rubber. They may look and feel much like the glass balls and get pulled into the juggling rotation, but they are not as critical and can be dropped when necessary and picked up later.

Ownership

If you look at your job as a manager and a leader as if it were its own standalone business, you will begin to feel a sense of ownership that drives entrepreneurs and small business owners to greatness. It's a simple but powerful and often overlooked viewpoint that is a strong complement to passion and focus.

A small business owner has a group identity: products and/or services, suppliers, customers, and employees. At any point in time, one or many of these has a problem that needs fixing or a situation that has developed that will impact your results negatively. For instance, if a supplier fails to deliver a shipment of products that is critical to the customer base, the owner can't just say sorry and expect there to be no fallout. Customers won't stand for it and will go elsewhere. The owner understands that the problem may or may not have been his fault, but it doesn't matter: A solution must be found.

It is extremely rare that a company succeeds without a strong sense of employee and manager ownership. Yet in most companies, many groups and individuals feel somewhat disconnected from the overall success or failure of the broader organization, as though they don't own their part of the business. A lack of ownership can lead to anonymity—where no one will pin a failure on you or your team, and conversely you will not be recognized for your successes. Anonymity can be a dangerous thing, so don't fall into the trap. Even if your manager or company executives do not recognize you the way you deserve, rise above that and drive for a sense of ownership on your team (and the resulting accountability and recognition). Your employees will feel more fulfilled, and your results will go up.

Embrace this level of ownership and take full responsibility for your own actions and outputs. Then infuse the same ownership into your employees—where they each own their individual business that is tied to the other businesses on the team and in the company, and they know their inputs, outputs, and goals and are empowered to find a way to achieve those goals. If all the team members and the manager feel they are responsible for their own business and this ownership is leveraged by focus and passion, success will be that much closer.

JOHN MALANOWSKI

THE IMPORTANCE OF LEADERSHIP TALENT BENCH STRENGTH IN BUSINESS MODEL RENEWAL

John Malanowski is vice president of human resources for North Atlantic Consumer Products for Kimberly-Clark Corporation, which is home to some of the world's most recognized and trusted consumer brands, including Huggies, Pull-Ups, Kotex, Depend, Kleenex, Cottonelle, Scott, Andrex, and Scottex. In his role, John has direct responsibility for the delivery of human capital strategies and programs for the company's $9.5 billion North Atlantic Personal Care and Family Care businesses and the U.S., Canadian, and European consumer sales forces, marketing services, and Kimberly-Clark's Global Nonwovens businesses. Prior experience includes serving in senior human resources roles in multiple companies, including Raytheon Company, Fidelity Investments, and Engage Media.

John Malanowski
Vice President, Human Resources
Kimberly-Clark Corporation, North Atlantic Consumer Products

John, you have been in human resources for decades. Tell me a bit about your work aligning human capital with the requirements of organizational goals.

I think that one of the biggest contributions that any human resource professional can make to an organization in terms of human capital alignment is in the area of workforce planning. I once worked for an organization that stopped all hiring for several years due to an industry downturn. Consequently, when the industry recovered, the organization did not have a sufficient number of experienced employees in place to support the business growth plans. In addition, the existing workforce highlighted a significant gap in the 6 to 15 years of experience demographic of the company. After mapping our existing workforce demographic, including projected attrition, we began a companywide effort that resulted in recruiting 10,000-plus new employees for several consecutive years. If we had approached hiring without looking at the existing workforce skills and demographic profile, we would not have achieved our goals. In addition, the company implemented a formal workforce planning function in the HR organization that is continually forecasting both internal and external labor requirements against its five-year operating plans.

Let's shift the focus slightly to leadership. What role do leaders play in ensuring the effectiveness of the efforts you described in your last answer?

Leadership was key to both identifying the problem and understanding the implications of having an available workforce with the skills and competencies required to respond to industry changes and meeting business plan growth goals. In this case, the leaders took a holistic approach to understanding the problem and painting a compelling vision, through facts and data, to support the need to launch a companywide hiring initiative. Through these efforts, leaders at all levels in the organization were involved in the hiring effort. They all understood the business implications of not having a workforce to meet both their individual and organizational goals.

Many companies are feeling the need to reinvent their businesses to respond to the disruptions in many industries. Do leaders need to reinvent themselves to help with this, or is it a matter of applying tried-and-true principles of leadership in different ways? (In other words, is next-generation leadership the same as last-generation leadership?)

Smart business leaders are constantly reinventing themselves to lead, anticipate, or mitigate the constant disruptions or changes in industry today. Globalization and technological change have put businesses under pressure to respond to market shifts and consumer preferences faster than ever before. The tried-and-true principles of leadership work only when leaders have adapted themselves and their leadership styles to what is effective in today's environment. With that said, the tried-and-true principles of leadership—e.g., not compromising on talent decisions, acting swiftly by unmistakable actions to deal with change, modeling accountability, and being a rock in the face of adversity—always work.

Transformational leadership has received a lot of press over the years. How would you describe the difference between transformational leadership and transactional leadership? What role do you think each plays in situations in which companies find it necessary to modify their business models?

Transactional leaders maintain the status quo and don't easily recognize the competitive threats and external factors that can quickly erode a business model. Transactional leaders work well when an organization has an operate-for-cash or low-growth business model. Transformational leaders, on the other hand, act with speed in separating the business issues that are beyond their control from those they can do something about. Transformational leaders then drive change by visible leadership. People emulate their leaders. Successful transformations are built around relentless focus on a few broad strategies, the right organization structure, top talent, and engaging frontline leaders in the need for change. Transformational leaders know how to pull each of these levers through experience. Not moving as fast as you should can lessen competitiveness.

Can you think of any examples of transformational leaders who successfully helped move an organization to a new business model? What are some of the specific things they did to make this happen?

Seventy percent of all change efforts fail. Seventy percent of those failures are due to organizational issues, largely employee resistance to change and management behavior not supportive of the change. To that end, one of the most important things that a transformational leader does to move an organization forward is to remove "blockers," i.e., people in key positions who do not possess the skills or willingness or perceive the need to move to a new business model. Given the rate and speed of change of competitive pressures, transformational leaders move on blockers for these reasons. I have seen several efforts fail because leaders relied on talent not equipped to move an organization forward.

In your career as a human resource executive, what have been some of your key learnings related to helping develop leaders of the future?

First, learning as a leader should never cease. Great leaders seek out big problems as opportunities to continue to differentiate themselves and hone their leadership skills. The leader who creates a compelling vision for change and models the behavior that is critical for success will be a catalyst for change and have a followership that can transcend organizations and generations.

Are there any final words of advice you can provide to managers and executives who are experiencing significant organizational transitions?

Don't hesitate to confront the transition head on. Change brings opportunity. Be the change that you want to see happen in your organization and lead from the front.

REFERENCES

Beller, Margo, "Dell a Different Business from 5 Years Ago: CEO," CNBC.com, June 29, 2011.

Bennis, Warren. *On Becoming a Leader,* Addison Wesley, 1994

Espin, Vicki, "Emotionally Intelligent Leadership," *Training Journal,* May 2010, pp. 67–70.

Facenda, Vanessa L., "Cowboy Culture/GE Mentality," *Retail Merchandiser,* August 2002, pp. 23–27.

Foust, Dean, "Where Headhunters Fear to Tread," *BusinessWeek,* September 14, 2009, pp. 42–44.

HBR Interview, "Being More Productive," *Harvard Business Review,* May 2011, pp. 82–87.

Hindo, Brian, and Brian Grow, "Six Sigma: So Yesterday? In an Innovation Economy, It's No Longer a Cure-All," *BusinessWeek,* June 11, 2007, p. 11.

Kotter, John, P., "What Leaders Really Do," *Harvard Business Review,* May–June 1990, pp. 103–112.

Lashinsky, Adam, "How Jobs Transformed Apple," CNNMoney.com, November 5, 2009.

McCarroll, Thomas, "A Builder, Not a Slasher," *TIME,* November 8, 1993, p. 63.

Mingis, Ken, "Michael Dell Returns as CEO at Namesake Company; Rollins Out," *Computerworld,* January 31, 2007.

Nye, Joseph S., Jr., "Contextual Intelligence," *Leadership Excellence,* January 2011, p. 11.

Rowe, Glenn, and Mehdi Hossein Nejad, "Strategic Leadership: Short-Term Stability and Long-Term Viability," *Ivey Business Journal* online, September–October 2009.

Savage, Anika, and Michael Sales, "The Anticipatory Leader: Futurist, Strategist and Integrator," *Strategy and Leadership,* 2008, vol. 36, no. 6, pp. 28–34.

Schultz, Howard, *Onward: How Starbucks Fought for Its Life without Losing Its Soul*, Rodale, 2011.

Smith, Brien N., Ray V. Montagno, and Tatiana N. Kuzmenko, "Transformational and Servant Leadership: Content and Contextual Comparisons," *Journal of Leadership and Organizational Studies*, Spring 2004, pp. 80–89.

Symonds, William, Geoffrey Smith, and Paul Judge, "Fisher's Photofinish: George Fisher Is Exiting as CEO: Can Anyone Turn Kodak Around?" *BusinessWeek*, June 21, 1999, p. 34.

Walter, Frank, Michael S. Cole, and Ronald H. Humphrey, "Emotional Intelligence: Sine Qua Non of Leadership or Folderol?" *Academy of Management Perspectives*, February 2011, pp. 45–59.

CHAPTER 7

Dynamic Strategy, Business Design, and Structural Alignment

When a strategy or business model is envisioned, it is like a preliminary prototype that will be refined and shaped over time. Henry Mintzberg referred to this process as "crafting" strategy, using the image of a master artisan as an analogy to the process of strategy building (Figure 7-1). A sculptor begins work on a piece of pottery within an initial concept but allows it to morph as new ideas emerge or flaws in the original design become apparent (the flaws sometimes even become part of the final product). Similarly, a strategist has to recognize that strategies and business models are rarely perfect at their inception and should be able to be tilted as required to move toward the higher-level goals and vision. Also, the very fact that numerous people in an organization are required to implement a strategy suggests that there will be different interpretations, sometimes on a day-to-day basis, of the best way to move toward the vision. The only way to handle this in a rapidly changing world is to accept real-time strategy making: dynamic strategy. The end results are emergent or consequential strategies.

Sometimes people confuse a strategy with a goal or a vision. The strategy is the plan of action, whereas the goal is the end result of that plan. An overemphasis on the strategy can obstruct the attainment of the goal. Here is an analogy. When my kids were little, my husband and I decided to drive to the Grand Canyon on a family vacation. Since we are just a few hours north of Chicago, we thought it would be interesting to take Route 66 as a nostalgic tour through old America. This historic highway spawned a TV show in the 1960s (*Route 66*) and received lyrical tributes ("get their

FIGURE 7-1 ➤ Learn to craft strategy

kicks on Route 66"). Unfortunately, we discovered that Route 66 no longer existed in its entirety, sometimes merging with other roadways and at other times stopping completely. (It was decommissioned in the 1980s.) If we had continued solely with Route 66 (the strategy), we never would have arrived at the Grand Canyon (our goal).

I have experienced this phenomenon with several clients. They may continue pursuing a particular customer acquisition approach, a product-development effort, or a cost-cutting measure long after it has begun to deviate from the goal. A dynamic strategy should be recalibrated constantly to refocus it toward a goal as environmental changes continue to occur. However, the focus should be on a limited number of pivotal goals whose accomplishment will drive the desired renewal of the business model.

I am not saying that goals alone will make strategies happen, and simply calling a goal a strategy doesn't work either. We've all listened to politicians making statements such as "My strategy is to create jobs" and "My plan is to balance the budget." Those aren't strategies; they're goals (or perhaps platitudes). Good strategies should acknowledge the challenges that will be faced in reaching goals and describe a plan to overcome them.

Dynamic strategy and business model renewal require adaptable leadership and a proactive culture. It won't happen as a result of fill-in-the-blanks templates, a flashy matrix, or complicated management models. It requires a change in organizational and leadership mindsets. Make no mistake: Goals, strategies, and business models must work in concert even though it is impossible to eliminate ambiguity. You must have the focus and determination to make them work.

BIG PICTURE THINKING MUST COEXIST WITH NUTS-AND-BOLTS PROFICIENCY

Charles Darwin frequently is quoted as saying: "It is not the strongest of the species that survive, nor the most intelligent, but the one most responsive to change." But there's more to it than that. Change is not necessarily good or bad, nor is acceptance of or resistance to change right or wrong. The reality is that change happens around us all the time and we must pick and choose which changes to react to and which to put on the back burner or ignore. Earlier I talked about both constancy of purpose (built to last and stick to your knitting) and major change initiatives (disruptive innovations) as being important but not magic bullets. There are times when either or both are appropriate.

For most of the twentieth century, General Motors was the biggest company in the most important industry in the world. It revolutionized the automotive field time and again. Then it filed for bankruptcy on June 1, 2009. It's a sort of paradox that the more successful a company is, the harder it is for that company to change to continue the success.

Most competitive advantages are not sustainable or permanent; old and new competitors continually try to take the advantage away from you. Throughout business, change is happening everywhere; some call it reinventing, some call it innovating, and some call it repositioning. *BusinessWeek* called organizations that adjust to change with relative ease corporate chameleons. The concept of a chameleon is interesting. Many species change their color to blend in with the surroundings as a form of camouflage. However, the change is not significant enough to survive in a dramatically different ecosystem. Therefore, chameleons can use camouflage to survive relatively smaller environmental changes whereas evolution may be necessary to respond to more significant change. Also, it's worth noting that being a chameleon may be contextually appropriate if the firm's fundamental approach is to be a "fast follower" but not if it strives to be a technological leader.

Metaphorically speaking, the same thing is true for businesses. The degree of corporate adaptation may be linked to the degree of environmental change. A few years ago, when *BusinessWeek* published the article on corporate chameleons, it cited digital music kiosks at Starbucks as an example. That move was consistent with $4 lattes and the unconventional passion for Starbucks as "the third place." But after the Great Recession, which forced store closings, employee layoffs, and an increased emphasis on cost cutting and efficiency measures, the ecosystem changed dramatically. Starbucks was competing with McDonald's and Dunkin' Donuts and focusing on supply chain improvements, operational standardization, real-time data analysis, and sophisticated marketing research. Changes are happening again with the return of Howard Schultz as CEO.

There are differences between structuring organizations for stability and structuring them for flexibility. Bureaucracies are built to reduce surprises. Processes and procedures are designed and fine-tuned to become ever more efficient and reliable in doing the same thing over and over. That simplifies the decision process but makes flexibility a harder goal to reach. The potential resistance to change must be addressed; this is explored in Chapter 8.

AN ITERATIVE PLANNING PROCESS

To link long-term and short-term thinking, an iterative planning process is useful. The vision will spawn a series of strategic goals or initiatives (in this case driven by the growth initiatives discussed in Chapter 2). Each strategic goal will have one or more high-level strategies with some level of detail in the action plans. (A brief discussion of Komatsu's links between vision and strategies appears later in this chapter.) However, the action plans will be refined and redefined into annual operating plans (AOPs) that vary with the specific environmental circumstances. Over some period of time the vision and strategic goals will be for the most part consistent and stable; the action plans will be more dynamic. This is shown in Figure 7-2.

FIGURE 7-2 ➤ Linking vision and strategies

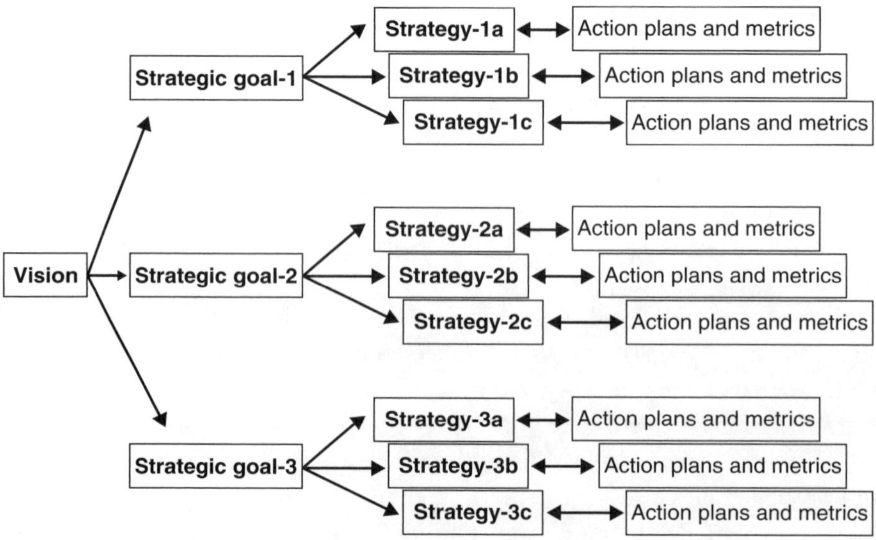

Although there is no magic to the approach presented above, it provides a starting point to keep a vision front and center while allowing recalibration on a short-term (say, six months to two years) basis. Here are questions to think through in developing the strategies and/or action plans (see Figure 7-3, where the wording and order of the questions are slightly different):

1. Where are you now? (the context from domain 1, augmented and updated as required by a particular type of plan)
2. Where do you want to go in the long term? (your strategic vision, long-term goals, and strategies informed through foresight efforts)
3. What are you going to do in this plan to come closer to your long-term vision? (objectives)
4. What actions will help you accomplish the objectives? (tactics or action plan)
5. How will you implement, track, and evaluate results? (metrics and measurements)

The process is not necessarily linear; some companies may start with the long-term vision (step 2) and move on to data gathering (step 1) or go back and forth between steps as new information emerges. However, all the steps generally are covered in some manner. The metrics and measurements in the final step over time continue to provide inputs for the first step.

FIGURE 7-3 ➤ An ongoing planning process

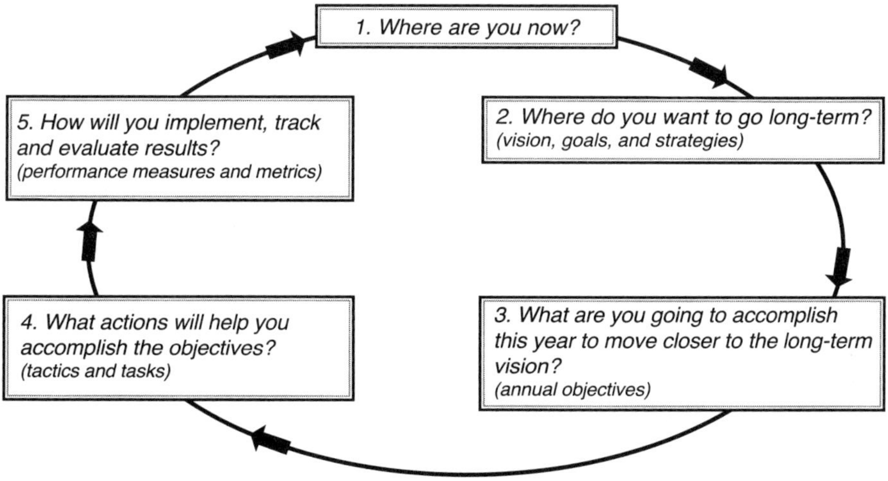

Where Are You Now?

Throughout the book several issues related to strategic thinking have been highlighted, particularly the TIME analysis and internal assessments that were part of domain 1. Now I want to link that to the more detailed analyses required for shorter-term (business) plans.

Examine how well various products, services, and revenue streams performed over time and relative to the prior plan. Look at the market share and financial and other numeric or statistical indicators of performance. Here it is important to learn where profits are rising or falling over time, how customers are being won or lost, and why overall performance is improving or getting worse.

In addition, reflect on questions like the ones listed below to provide qualitative data that could highlight problems and opportunities to be addressed in the plan.

Your market knowledge and positioning

- How well have you been performing in your current market in terms of revenue, growth, and profitability over the last three years?
- Which segments of the market have been growing? Declining?
- What new segments are emerging?
- What segments are most attractive in light of the growth initiatives in the organizational strategy?
- What is your current market share?
- What has been the trend in market share over the last three years?
- What is your position vis-à-vis the competition?

Your operational status

- What has been the performance and trends in supply chain efficiency?
- What has been the three-year trend of product, service, and revenue stream quality?
- What assets are underutilized?
- What assets are obsolete?
- Have investment and cost allocation procedures been revisited within the last five years?
- Are current IT and technology systems up to date?
- How effectively have personnel capabilities been developed and deployed?

- What revenue-generation efforts have failed in the last three years because of inefficient processes, rigid organizational structures, or misaligned culture?
- Has the value of repair services changed (as a result of cost increases, repair person efficiency, technological change, self-service, or any other reason)?

Your products, services, and revenue streams

- In what stage of the product life cycle are the products? Which are in the beginning phases, which are in growth, which are mature, and which are candidates for elimination? Does this confirm your prior thinking about reinforcement, renewal, and retirement?
- What does the name of the product imply? Can it be branded (or rebranded)?
- Which features or products are distinguishable by the customer?
- For each feature, ask "so what?" to identify the benefits from the customer's point of view.
- Are the products supplied through intermediaries (e.g., dealers)? If so, the analysis of features, benefits, and/or values should be handled in two steps.
- If a numeric rating were given to product quality (with 1 being low and 7 being high), what would that rating be? Would the rating be the same for all customer segments? For all products?
- What does each item contribute to sales and profits? To customer satisfaction? Can some of the items be pruned?
- How do the various items' rates of return compare with the company's overall rate of return?
- Are product designs conducive to an efficient manufacturing process?
- What are the engineering costs for product development, product engineering, and manufacturing engineering?
- What are the unit breakeven sales volumes for the products?
- Are product guarantees competitive?
- What would happen if the products were more standardized? More customized?

Pricing

- Have significant amounts of business been lost because of prices?
- Are errors frequently made in pricing?
- What is the perceived cost of buying the product or service?

- Is the company a price leader or a price follower?
- What is the pricing policy of the company?
- What types of discounts are offered? How does that compare with the competition?

The sales force

- Is the current sales force structure appropriate for achieving your objectives?
- Are the target customers being reached in the most effective and efficient manner?
- How effective have the product training and sales training been?
- What sales tools do the salespeople actually use to sell?
- Has the sales force been taught how to help customers visualize the benefits of the offerings?

The distribution strategy

- What are the channels of distribution? What percentage of the product sales are through each type of intermediary?
- What is the company's relationship with intermediaries (distributors, agents, retailers, etc.)?
- What are distribution costs as a percentage of sales?
- How does the company's policy for distributor or retailer margins compare with those of competitors?
- What has been the recent history of stockouts, substitutes, and back orders?

Trend and event dynamics

- What technological changes are likely to occur during this planning cycle?
- What leading indicators correspond with sales, and what do they suggest?
- What are the basic trends and changes in the economy?
- Are there regulatory or political forces that could affect sales during this planning cycle?

Where Do You Want to Go in the Long Term?

The function and relevance of a vision has been discussed at several points in the book. (In Chapter 6 it was compared to a future annual report.) The vision statement helps keep plans aligned and focused on a general (albeit occasionally a bit fuzzy) direction. It often highlights the core capabilities the company has along with what it needs to develop. As Gary Hamel and C. K. Prahalad explained in their classic *Harvard Business Review* article "Strategic Intent," strategies and shorter-term plans can be guided by the overarching vision. (But even the vision may need to be reexamined periodically, as will be discussed in a moment.)

Komatsu, a Japanese manufacturer of bulldozers, developed a strategic vision of being a global player in earthmoving equipment; in essence, this was a vision of beating Caterpillar. In 1964 the company's president, Ryoichi Kawai, announced the strategic intent of catching up to and surpassing Caterpillar. This required a series of intermediate-term strategies that focused on the immediate problems and opportunities Komatsu had to respond to in the process of achieving its long-term goal.

In the 1960s, Komatsu was about a third the size of Caterpillar, limited to one product line (small bulldozers), and scarcely represented outside of Japan. When Komatsu wanted to discourage Caterpillar from entering the Japanese market in the 1960s, its strategy was to protect its home market through various product improvements, cost reductions, and new product development through licensing agreements. In the early 1970s, Komatsu's challenge was to develop export markets. Since it was not yet strong enough to compete head to head with Caterpillar, it chose to export to markets in which Caterpillar was weak. Then, in the late 1970s, Komatsu felt prepared to compete against Caterpillar in the U.S. market. Table 7-1 presents a simplified summary of the strategies it used over a 20-year period to move toward its vision.

Table 7-1

Komatsu's Long-Term Vision: Beat Caterpillar

Date	Corporate Challenge	Activities
Early 1960s	• Protect Komatsu's home market against Caterpillar	• Licensing deals with Cummins Engine, International Harvester, and Bucyrus-Erie
Mid-1960s	• Begin quality improvement efforts	• Several quality and cost reduction programs
1960s to early 1970s	• Build export markets	• Komatsu Europe established • Service departments to assist newly industrializing countries
Late 1970s	• Create new products and markets	• Future and Frontiers program to identify new businesses based on society's needs and company's know-how • Enters U.S. market

Note how the company started with a long-term vision or direction: become a more dominant global player than Caterpillar. Then, on an intermediate-term basis, it focused on the current problems and opportunities that affected its ability to move toward its vision. In other words, the organization focused on the steps that had to be taken at the current point in time to move closer to the future picture of the company. Each year, Kawai defined a clear and specific operating priority that used Caterpillar's performance as a competitive target and benchmark. This approach worked well, and the company grew from a tiny local competitor with poor quality to a serious global challenger to Caterpillar.

By 1989 the environmental context had changed. Worldwide demand for construction equipment was down, and competition was up. The vision of surpassing Caterpillar was not as inspirational as it had been in 1964, and inertia began to set in. Tetsuya Katada, Komatsu's president (the third to follow Kawai), realized that an exclusive focus on the best practices of one competitor had caused the company to stop thinking about strategic choices. He told his managers that he wanted "everyone to stop concentrating simply on catching up with Caterpillar" (Bartlett and Ghoshal, 1994) and challenged the managers to seek out new opportunities. During the next three years there was almost 40 percent growth in Komatsu's nonconstruction equipment business.

It's clear that the vision has to define a desired future, help coordinate strategies, and inspire employees. And it's not always measurable. As Albert Einstein said, "Not everything that can be counted counts and not everything that counts can be counted." Although the vision is not a one-time forever statement, it should last for multiple planning cycles and act as the glue for multiple initiatives. However, like any internal directive, it should be open for reexamination if the context changes. Remember that the ability to read and adapt to signals in the internal and external environment increases a company's success in an era of risk and instability.

What Are You Going to Accomplish during This Planning Cycle?

The third step requires you to answer the question: What are you going to accomplish with this plan to move one step closer from where you are now to where you want to be in the future? In this section you identify how you will develop, test, and refine the growth initiatives discussed in Chapter 2. Begin by defining the results you want to obtain, as objectives, using terms that are SMART:

Specific
Measurable
Attainable
Results-oriented
Time-bound

Specific objectives are quantitative, such as a given percentage increase in market share, unit growth in volume, or a specified number of product trials. *Measurable* refers to the ability to track results. Having a goal of, say, reaching 32 percent of scientists with artificial limbs is specific but would be very difficult to measure. Being *attainable* is subjective. Goals by their very nature require a change in the status quo, but if they are impossible to attain, they are really dreams. The *results-oriented* criterion is perhaps the most important. If the objectives specify the results (rather than the activities) you are striving to achieve, they accomplish two things. First, they provide direction for the plan; second, they become a metric against which to compare actual performance. When to compare these results metrics against actual performance is bound by the final criterion, *time.*

Objectives can be stated in terms of units or dollars (revenue and/or margin), market share, customer satisfaction level, and so on. Emphasis should be given to the specific target customers you will focus on; this may include customer acquisition and retention goals. Typically, the objective starts with a verb (*increase, maintain, solidify*, etc.) acting on a specific desired outcome (repeat purchases, new trial, sales volume/revenue, etc.) for a stated market (profiled market segment or account) within a specified time period (typically a year). An example objective is shown in Figure 7-4.

FIGURE 7-4 ➤ Example objective

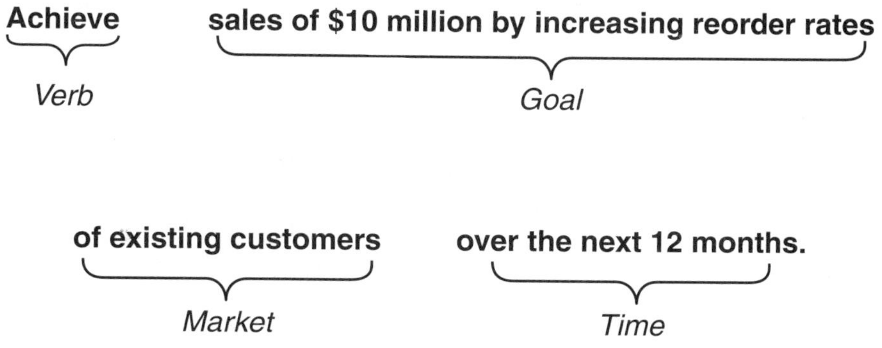

Target Market

What type of customer or group of customers is most likely to buy the product? Resist the temptation to put every possible prospect into the description. You want to focus on the "ideal" customer: the one who has the greatest need for your business and its products, services, and revenue streams; perceives value in them; and is likely to respond to your value proposition efforts. The profile not only clarifies who you are trying to reach but also implies who you are not going after. The needs of this target customer drive your product design efforts, pricing, channel decisions, and operational efforts. (If people who are not in your target market want to buy the product, that's fine as long as it doesn't require a change in the factors just listed.) No product can be all things to all people. Trying to achieve that results in a diluted product and/or a diluted customer value proposition.

Planning FACTS

To help you be more effective in steps 3 and 4, I want to introduce you to the FACTS of planning. The acronym FACTS is a mnemonic for some of the most common generic tools of planning and implementation: flowcharts, action maps, checklists, templates, and schedules (see Figure 7-5). These are tools that can help you with tactical plans and implementation.

Flowcharts are diagrammatic representations of operations, activities, and decisions, with symbols used to indicate the various phases of a process. Stage-gate processes, activity networks such as critical path and PERT (Project Evaluation and Review Technique), and other step-by-step sequences of these steps are examples. *Action maps* are visual or textual

FIGURE 7-5 ➤ Planning FACTS

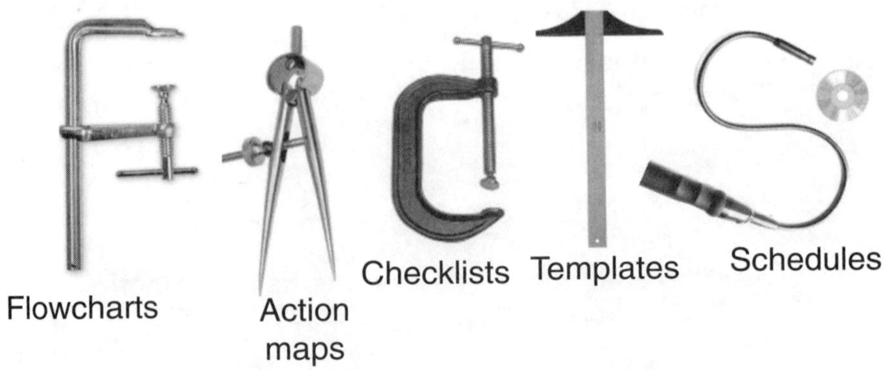

representations of future direction. Longer-term maps such as technology road maps, scenario plans, and portfolio strategies delineate less-detailed activities and decisions. Shorter-term maps such as verbal descriptions of activities, tactics, and financials provide more complex details for implementation. *Checklists* are very basic listings of tasks but can be quite powerful because of their simplicity. Checklists of important standard tasks to be completed before a product launch or pilot project can reduce the probability of a critical piece of a plan falling short. *Templates* are generally simple fill-in-the-blanks worksheets. Similar to checklists, they help minimize the chance of overlooking an important element of a plan. *Schedules*, the last item in the FACTS toolbox, are essentially annotated calendars with specific individuals assigned specific dates to complete required activities. As a result, they are necessary for assigning responsibility and deadlines for the implementation of plans. Although any of these tools can be used at any point in the planning process, flowcharts and action maps are most useful for analysis and process, whereas checklists, templates, and schedules are important tools for compliance (with internal requirements) and implementation.

How Are You Going to Accomplish Your Objectives?

The fourth step of the process details the activities and tactics expected to accomplish the stated objectives. What are you going to stop doing, continue doing, or begin doing to make progress toward the vision? Keep in mind the role of objectives versus tactics (similar to the discussion of goals versus strategies). Since the objectives are the desired results of the plan, they are more concrete, whereas the tactics should be more fluid and responsive to the environment. In most situations flexing should happen in the tactics rather than in the objectives. The relative stability of objectives married with the flexibility of tactics yields a dynamically stable operational plan. This is similar to the relative stability of vision and goals married with the flexibility of strategies, yielding a dynamically stable strategic plan.

This step involves executing against your growth initiatives in a way that is consistent with the long-term goals and vision.

What Are Your Metrics for Tracking Results?

The highest-level metric for your plan is the attainment of the results you specified in your objectives. (Results refer to the R in the SMART acronym.) From a strategic perspective, it's also useful to include metrics on the long-term health of the organization. However, you don't want to wait until the end of the year (or whatever the planning cycle is) to measure progress. Rather, build into the plan checkpoints where you can determine whether you are on track or whether corrective action should be taken.

LEGO has been using a monthly meeting of senior managers not only to share results from the current month but also to revisit the next 12-month forecast. Some companies, particularly in Europe, have created more formalized *rolling forecasts*. Each quarter they look at the next four quarters to update them with new information on an ongoing basis and continually reinforce the link between past, present, and future. Although this occasionally may cause changes to the objectives in step 3, it does that from the perspective of a future change (two to four quarters out) to allow time for realignment. That also enables leaders to communicate with employees about results while reinforcing the long-term intent and the relationship of the action plan to the vision or strategic goals with which it is aligned.

DYNAMIC STRATEGY AND BUSINESS MODEL RENEWAL

How can organizations be dynamically responsive to a changing environment? First, recognize that there are no magic bullets. Use tools, techniques, and models to inform your thinking but don't expect them to make the decision for you. Second, focus on pivotal goals that drive you toward the future you envision. Avoid fluff and extreme fuzziness. Decide which goals to focus on actively and which to table. Third, build a culture in which change readiness is dynamic and proactive so that necessary recalibrations are viewed as business as usual rather than formal change programs. Fourth, think in portfolio terms when considering business model renewal and expect dynamic strategy to occur in each business model. Fifth, remember that goals and strategies without actions are wishes and dreams. Leaders must go beyond rhetoric to design a way to coordinate actions that truly results in progress. Sixth, practice the wisdom of and. Remember that today's decisions can and will affect future outcomes. Be prepared to respond to current challenges without losing sight of long-term goals.

SCOTT LINGREN

CRACKING THE REAL-WORLD CODE FOR LINKING STRATEGY WITH IMPLEMENTATION

Scott Lingren has been a technology executive for over 20 years, working in corporate strategy, business development, marketing, turnarounds and transformations, and global general management while leading global teams at Dell, Nokia, Clearwire, AT&T, and most recently Freescale, where he led a successful turnaround and initial public offering. Scott is currently the director of corporate strategy and business transformation for Freescale Semiconductor. He has undergraduate and graduate business degrees from the University of Wisconsin–Madison and Edgewood College and lives with his wife, Theresa, in Austin, Texas.

Scott A. Lingren
Director of Corporate Strategy and Business Transformation
Freescale Semiconductor

Scott, you've been involved in strategy development and strategy execution for several organizations. What were some of the challenges you've faced in connecting the two?

Wow, there are a lot of issues to address in this question. My experience as a head of corporate strategy and as a group general manager has taught me that a lot of operational and implementation issues are fairly consistent across disparate industries and organizational structures. While many similar challenges exist within both very small start-up (or entrepreneurial) companies and larger corporations, my comments are geared more to the range of midsize companies (200-plus employees) up to the largest multinationals.

In many organizations, the stated corporate strategy is either vague or aspirational, more like a vision or mission statement than a strategic direction; it's parsed out in group-specific bits on a need-to-know basis like some sort of military secret or is simply not shared at all. Creating a clear and measurable strategic direction is step 1 (more like steps 1 through 20, but we'll keep things simple), followed by the steps needed to communicate and execute the strategy. Presuming for the sake of this discussion that a solid strategic plan has been created and has a significant level of traction with the top levels of the organization, the operational challenges of executing the strategy must be addressed. There are actually six issues I want to mention here.

First of all, buy-in: Since most of the individuals involved in executing a strategic plan were not personally involved in its creation, there is often an understandable and predictable lack of buy-in. Without this buy-in—this personal awareness of the strategy, its validity, and its relevance to their groups—most individuals will lack the conviction and focus needed to implement it successfully.

Leaders need to educate the groups on how this strategy was developed. When the individuals and groups that are implementing the strategy know the process, how they and their colleagues were involved (or ideally are currently involved if the strategy is still being formed), and how it is all relevant to their jobs and daily lives, the buy-in for the direction and the supporting goals (and how the company arrived at those goals) is much stronger. The sense of ownership will be higher—buy-in helps mitigate much of the feeling that the strategy was "not invented here"—and will lead to a much greater probability of success.

Next is communication: Since most individuals and groups spend little time thinking about strategic direction, the concepts and framework are often not familiar and may strike many as only platitudes, corporate-speak, or irrelevant to their own roles and success. Leadership must directly link the company vision/mission to the corporate strategy—to the corporate objectives—and then to the group-level metrics and measurements. Executives and managers, especially those who are directly involved in the strategy creation, may make the mistake of assuming others will see the linkage between high-level strategy and operational execution. Never presume that others will see all the dots, much less make the connection; leaders need to create a consistent, clear, seamless flow from vision through to measurement.

To the points on consistency and clarity of the communications, the strategy needs to be explained by the CEO to the entire company, then reiterated by the group GMs and reinforced by all managers. Management should host a review of the strategy so that all managers can ask questions, provide feedback, and further hone the messaging so that the key points and actions are clear, are consistent, and are relevant throughout the company.

That brings me to relevance and respect: The communication challenge I just talked about has the related challenge of relevance and respect embedded within it. Individuals will be consciously or subconsciously asking: How do the corporate and group strategies affect me and my group, and how will I and my organization be expected to affect the success of the strategy?

Leaders need to broaden the field of vision for their groups to provide the context for how the high-level strategy and individual goals are linked. This can be very challenging, since it is difficult to frame the total picture (changing dynamics in the market landscape, competitive pressures, investor expectations, short- and long-term goals, and so forth) and map it directly to individual areas of execution. Groups focus on their piece of the business, by definition, so they often don't see the broader picture—and in many ways shouldn't be expected to since they are paid to be successful in their respective areas of expertise. So there needs to be context for every goal and execution plan so that the management and the teams understand the relevance of the roles they are playing and the importance of their success to the success of the company strategy.

This is also a respect issue for employees. Many companies communicate only the simplest views of the strategic direction, choosing to leave out important details, the logic flow behind the decisions, the tough choices that had to be made, and the challenges the organization will face in trying to meet these challenges. This is a big mistake. Companies are not brands or buildings or families of products; they are groups of employees. So to severely limit the description of the strategy to the wider employee population, including how the strategy was developed and how it will be rolled out, is to severely limit the ability of your company to understand the strategy and its relevance to the individuals who will determine its success. Providing details of the process, the hard decisions, and the challenges and imperfections will show not only that senior management understands and is connected to the messy and difficult issues that every business faces but also that the employees are trusted with these insights and have the intelligence to apply them to their daily lives. Any organization that says its employees are the foundation of the company and wants to be successful in implementing its strategies must make the effort needed to provide clear and consistent details to the entire employee base. It should be no surprise that there is a direct correlation between companies that commit to that investment and the level of success they achieve in the marketplace.

My fourth point is positive pressure: Another of the challenges involved with implementing a strategy is a lack of positive pressure throughout the organization. The company will need a role (individual or group) that is objective, will challenge the businesses, and will provide pressure to keep the urgency and focus at a high level. They should be dispassionate and fact-based to challenge the groups regarding their inputs/outputs/plans/progress. This devil's advocate approach will poke at assumptions and approaches and provide enough pressure on the system to check the validity or scalability of plans. It will also determine how well they integrate with other plans across the organization and ultimately their probability of success.

This type of role is usually filled by a corporate strategy group for the overall implementation since they were probably deeply involved in the creation of the strategy and should have the field of vision to provide context—and thus relevance—across the entire company. At the group level a program manager can be the critical implementation steward to push for success during the rollout and will need the public support of his or her management to ensure the appropriate level of influence on the process.

Next I want to mention sandbagging: One additional challenge that emerges during strategy implementation and should be watched carefully by the program managers who are applying positive pressure is sandbagging. I am sure everyone is familiar with this idea of decreasing performance expectations in the hopes of greatly or more easily surpassing a lowered bar. In my experience sandbagging is minimal during the creation of the strategy, since the aspirational level is high and the exposure of senior executives to one another and the CEO is obvious.

Everyone wants to be a part of setting challenging, "feel-good" goals for the entire company.

Sandbagging happens more during the implementation phase, when the reality of the operational challenges takes hold, and provides an environment where it is tempting to introduce excuses, delays, and exceptions—real or invented—to lower the expectations for a group. Leaders may consciously or subconsciously pull back from goals they need to support, knowing it will lead directly to related performance objectives for them and their teams. This limits the potential of the group or company if the leader allows sandbagging and is not stretching far enough to push his or her teams. Leaders at all levels must gauge their own actions to ensure they are setting the right example and must watch the managers within their organizations carefully for signs of softened standards.

And finally, anticorporate resistance: My final comment regarding the challenges faced in implementing a strategy is related to the common and natural resistance most groups feel toward corporate-driven initiatives. Strategies, from the way they are worded to the executives who communicate them, are often viewed by the operational groups as a corporate mandate created by disconnected suits in their ivory towers. Many of us have heard statements (or have had thoughts ourselves) like "They just sit in meetings all day," "They don't really understand what is going on," "They don't run the business, I do," and "More projects from the corporate goons." This is a huge challenge and threatens the successful implementation of the strategy if it gets out of hand.

Although much has been written on the subject of the "us versus them" syndrome businesses feel about corporate roles and it is unlikely this dynamic will ever go away completely, there are ways to minimize the impact. Working through the challenges I just discussed of buy-in, communication, and relevance and respect should provide some measure of relief, so investing in the preparation for those initial stages will pay off quickly. From the corporate side it's important to assemble a strategy team that has real-world business operations experience (as general managers, preferably). They need to know the challenges of executing a strategy and have an appreciation for the "anticorporate" perceptions of being on the business side. Although one of the roles of corporate strategy is to challenge the businesses on their execution plans and progress, they should also acknowledge that the businesses will run themselves since they are the experts.

Strategy is always evolving, especially in rapidly changing industries. What specific actions did you take to connect long-term strategy with short-term plans and day-to-day operations?

First, the long-term strategy, the middle- and short-term goals, and the daily operations must be tightly aligned, using consistent words and metrics to make the linkages obvious. By making the investment up front to overcome the initial challenges of strategy implementation—securing buy-in for the strategy throughout the organization, communicating the objectives clearly and thoroughly, making the goals relevant at every level, and showing respect to all employees—the company is already in a very strong position to successfully drive the day-to-day operations.

I believe an absolute requirement for operationalizing any strategy is to have systems and processes in place to measure the metrics and milestones. A broader way to look at this is to ensure strong overall operational governance: establishing key metrics up front and getting buy-in, creating clear and concise scorecards/dashboards, and mapping reviews to existing forums (operations meetings, senior executive discussions, group-level and company-level sessions). The challenge is to create a relatively small set of metrics that are the success predictors for the company. Establishing consistent measurement, using publicly shown and discussed reports, and linking actions to the gaps and milestones will drive behaviors and priorities to achieve success. And by including strategic and operational goals in every communication—at the group and company level, CEO updates, analyst discussions, earnings calls—all internal and external communications will be consistent and become self-reinforcing.

Have any of the strategy changes you have initiated or been involved with been accompanied by business model changes? Can you talk about that a bit?

Absolutely. Since strategy is a combination of relatively static, long-term aspirational goals plus flexible adaptations to changing market conditions, many business models require updating as a result. One that comes immediately to mind is Clearwire Technologies, where I was heavily involved in driving a changing strategy and business model.

Clearwire Technologies, which specialized in the creation of broadband wireless networks and services, faced the decision to alter the business model as a result of both proactive and reactive factors. The proactive changes resulted from exploratory ways to more quickly monetize the company's deep, rare wealth of expertise in making broadband wireless networks work, a capability that is challenging enough in theory and is actually much more difficult in practice. The reactive changes were driven by the acknowledgment that Clearwire's potential customers, the Internet service providers, highly valued the wireless Internet access that we provided but did not have the capital to purchase their own wireless networks, the expertise to run them efficiently, or the scale to operate them profitably. To take advantage of both the company's core competencies and the realities of an emerging marketplace, we needed to adjust our business model.

So Clearwire made a huge change to its business model, shifting from the design and creation of turnkey networks that would be sold outright to creating and running its own wholesale wireless networks and selling the access as a service to Internet service providers. This approach was far more capital-intensive and thus a riskier play for the investors, but the growth potential was much higher. Deciding what *not* to do was every bit as important as deciding what *to* do.

Over time we learned more and more about how our expertise could best be harnessed in the marketplace, and additional partners emerged who helped shape further changes to the business plan. We partnered to acquire underutilized but potentially lucrative licenses to wireless spectrum and spun off the equipment division to create a more pure network/service approach. The business model did not support the rapid expansion of networks tied to a standard consumer approach due to the high level of consumer price sensitivity and alternative options and to the cost of directly acquiring customers (advertising, branding, promotion, sales teams, physical stores/presence, and so forth). So while we briefly provided some marketing and brand awareness advertising directly to end users with the goal of driving demand to our ISP partners, we stayed true to our strategic approach of being a wholesale service provider primarily targeting businesses. Through a combination of proactive and reactive updates to the business model, Clearwire grew to be the largest provider of broadband Internet access in the world and to this day remains one of the largest players in this space.

Have you ever implemented a strategy that should not have worked but did? Or the reverse? What are some of the factors that caused that?

Sometimes all the facts, research, and feedback point in one direction while the instincts and vision of a leader point in another. One example of this that I did not directly create but did help implement took place at AT&T Wireless.

During the late 1990s, the CEO of AT&T's relatively new wireless company was Dan Hesse, a longtime AT&T veteran who is now better known as the CEO and commercial face of Sprint. The strategic challenge was to find a way to make cellular calling plans easier for end customers, with the goal of adding many new subscribers to the AT&T Wireless Services (AWS) network. At that time any cellular calls that were made from a network not owned by the subscriber's home company—called roaming—generated very high charges to the subscriber, discouraging many users from using their cell phones regularly and discouraging others from signing up for the service at all.

My understanding is that Mr. Hesse proposed the concept of a single set of rates for AWS cellular subscribers, regardless of network. The team's research and business models could not predict any sustainably successful scenario where AWS would add enough profitable new business to more than offset the cost of absorbing the roaming fees they would continue paying to their partners for roaming calls. But Hesse was undeterred. He was convinced in his gut that this was the future of cellular service and that AT&T Wireless needed to be the leader.

So with little or no business modeling proof that I was aware of to support the change, Hesse and his team proclaimed that AT&T Wireless would shift strategy and become the first to provide a single set of rates nationwide, providing a relatively predictable cost for AWS customers and effectively ending the uncertainty tied to roaming charges. At the time I, and many others, thought this was an absolutely brilliant marketing move ... and an absolutely insane business move.

It was not surprising that customer reaction was instantly and enthusiastically positive. The highly desirable but often costly and confusing service that cellular provided at the time was now much more clear and understandable. Customers joined AWS in record numbers, migrating from existing regional or national cellular carriers or starting service for the first time. The change in strategy was a huge success in the customers' eyes.

What I found to be very surprising was the chain reaction of unforeseen, or at least improbable, changes that this successful rate plan was forcing on the industry. The carriers that continued to pass roaming fees on to their customers were losing subscribers in droves, and many made the change to adopt plans similar to the AWS nationwide plan. This huge migration of new and existing users made it very difficult for carriers to continue charging extremely high rates for calls made on their networks and eventually led to the effective extinction of roaming charges.

In fairness, I am certain that the discussions and negotiations going on behind the scenes between the carriers were messy and rough and that the changes were not made easily or willingly. Some years later a similar strategic shift took place—the inclusion of long-distance calling in the base cellular rate plans—presumably driven by similar factors and causing the resulting changes within the industry. But it is the vision and the leap of faith that Dan Hesse and the AT&T Wireless team made and the resulting changes in consumer-buying behavior and industry practices—both foreseen and unforeseen by the strategy team—which I find so fascinating.

Here are the factors that I believe caused this to be successful:

- *Vision:* The CEO's strong sense of the industry direction, the role he wanted his company to play, and the best opportunity window.
- *Faith:* A belief among the senior leadership that they would overcome any obstacles that were not anticipated as part of the initial plan, that they could identify and remedy unforeseen factors as they emerged.
- *Support:* A board of directors who clearly believed in their leader and his team and would provide the investment and stewardship needed to make this risky move.

- *Muscle:* Behind-the-scenes work internally to prepare the company for the changes and implications of the new direction and externally with operating partners.
- *Focused and clear communications:* The teams chose a very succinct strategy change and provided very clear and concise messaging to employees and customers.

On the other hand, there are also examples of well-crafted strategies that failed during implementation. I have seen factors that are consistently present in a postmortem analysis of many of these types of failed implementations:

- Lack of strong, public resolve at the top levels: Senior leaders who are not consistent in what they say publicly versus what they do internally.
- Lack of vision and clear communications: Strategy that is not clearly tied to—and in the worst case is in conflict with—long-, middle-, and short-term metrics or operational imperatives.
- Lack of disciplined governance: Implementation plans that do not use metrics that are agreed upon or tied to known success predictors, measurement that is inconsistent or unclear, lack of action plans and owners, poor levels of accountability for results.
- Death by a thousand cuts: Managers who show a willingness to grant exceptions and deviations over and over and who fail to see that many complaints/issues/excuses seem very reasonable when taken in isolation but when combined undermine the operational foundation of the strategic changes, resulting in suboptimal results.
- Ego/fear: Leaders and managers who may have supported the strategic direction and changes at inception but feel threatened or micromanaged during the implementation.
- Lack of appropriate preparation and timing: An execution plan that was either rolled out too fast (created a heavy shock to the system: "organ rejection") or took too long, creating damage because of apathy or decreasing levels of relevance (they tried to prepare for every single possibility, get every scenario prewired, and get every

possible buy-in or tried to phase in too little at a time in a "boil the frog" attempt to implement changes that virtually no one felt).

- Organizational weakness: Implementation is when it all becomes real and may expose a lack of skills (technical, creative, adaptable, collaborative) in the organization that means it does not—or cannot—support the new direction; this may require key new personnel or leadership, new tools, training, changes to the environment or culture, alterations to the organization structure, or the scrapping of that strategic direction altogether.
- Distractions: The organization became distracted by opportunities that appeared overly attractive ("shiny, shiny") or by the tactics and fires that consume the daily operations of the business. This malady is especially true for public companies pressured to deliver an unbroken streak of gains each quarter.

In your opinion, is there a difference between strategy and tactics?

Absolutely. But one without the other leaves the total planning cycle incomplete at best, most likely damaged or suboptimal, and in some cases doomed before the start.

As described previously, the vision/mission and strategy must be directly linked to and reinforced by the operational tactics (metrics, reports, actions, and priorities).

What three things do you believe every manager should do to increase the probability of implementation success?

It is difficult to narrow this down to just three things, since strategic implementations are complex and thus require a commitment to a holistic set of actions. But if I had to highlight three areas that are mission-critical and are often overlooked or are assumed to take place naturally, they would be clear communications, regular measurement, and leadership by example.

- *Clear communications:* Tie vision/mission to strategy, to corporate goals, and to group goals and metrics and show how these goals are relevant to each employee and group.

- *Regular measurement:* Tie individual goals to group/corporate goals and strategy and scorecards/dashboards to clearly show consistent measurement, progress, and gaps. Focus on the most critical gaps (manage by exception), link the actions and outcomes to those gaps, and hold owners accountable for their results.
- *Leadership by example:* Make the strategic and related group goals a regular topic in team meetings, operational reviews, personnel reviews and development, project assignments, and cross-group communications. Capture best practices and celebrate successes. Do what you say you will do.

Do you have any other tips for successful implementation of strategies or business model changes?

I would not underestimate the commitment and investment needed by everyone in senior leadership and management to make the execution of a strategy successful. The preparation and rollout workload is on top of the regular challenges of the job and often occurs at times that seem the least convenient.

Carefully evaluate the challenges and reasons for failure I mentioned previously, expect that every one of these issues or problems will be a major factor, and plan for them in advance. Acknowledge up front that these things hit every leadership team in every industry no matter how good the strategies and the teams implementing them are. Work through the details of how you, your teams, and your partners must address each of the fail points in a consistent manner, with the goal of either neutralizing each problem or turning it to your advantage. Be ready for this. Get your teams ready for this. Surprise is the enemy; take the time to anticipate problems so you can get out in front of them.

Finally, I've put together a Strategic and Operational Planning Cycle document (Figure 7-6), which I've found personally valuable. I'd like to share it with your readers.

FIGURE 7-6 ➤ Strategic and operational planning cycle document

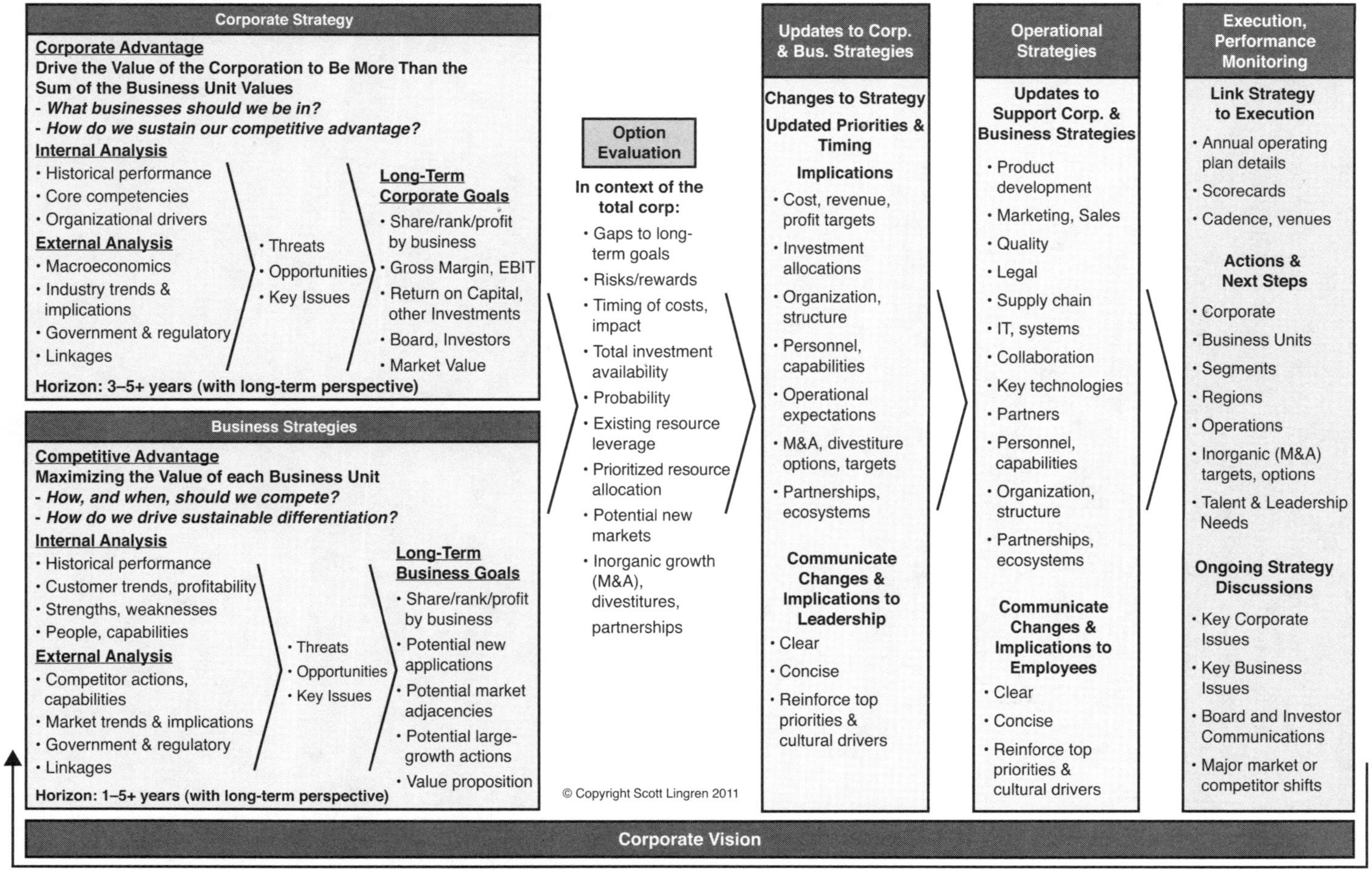

REFERENCES

Bartlett, Christopher A., and Sumantra Ghoshal, "From Strategic Intent to Corporate Purpose: The Remaking of Komatsu," *Harvard Business Review,* November–December 1994, p. 83.

"Business: Managing in the Fog; Corporate Planning," *The Economist*, February 28, 2009, pp. 67–68.

Hamel, Gary, and C. K. Prahalad, "Strategic Intent," *Harvard Business Review,* May–June 1989, pp. 63–76.

Hof, Robert D., and Michael Arndt, "How to Hit a Moving Target," *Business-Week*, August 21, 2006, p. 80.

CHAPTER 8

The People Side of Alignment: Culture and Organizational Change

There is an old saying that culture eats strategy for lunch. In other words, a strategy or business model that is inconsistent with an organization's culture has a high likelihood of failure. Modifications have to be made to the strategy and business model, the culture, or both.

The culture of an organization is essentially its personality. It is based on the core values of the firm, the experiences of the employees, and the expectations of internal and external constituents. Corporate culture is the invisible glue that holds companies together; it's "the way we do things around here"; it's the collective personality of the organization, consisting of beliefs, values, and behaviors. Strategy and culture influence each other, but one can be more dominant, and it's usually culture.

THE MONKEY PARABLE

There's a story floating around the Internet these days about culture. It's apparently derived from an anthropological study on learned behavior in rhesus monkeys conducted by G. R. Stephenson in the 1960s. There are subtle variations to what I'll call the Monkey Parable, but the basic theme is the same. It goes something like this.

Researchers put five monkeys into a cage; inside the cage is a banana hung on a string above a ladder. Before long, one of the monkeys attempts to climb the ladder to get the banana. Immediately the researchers spray all the other monkeys with cold water. They continue to do this every time a monkey goes after the banana. After a while, all the monkeys keep the other monkeys from trying to get the banana.

Next, the researchers remove one monkey and replace it with another. The new monkey makes a grab for the banana but is prevented from reaching it by the other monkeys. After several more attempts (and several more attacks from the other monkeys), the new monkey becomes assimilated into the "don't go after the banana" culture. Once that culture is established, the behavior continues each time a new monkey is introduced into the environment.

By the time all the original monkeys had been replaced, none of the current group had been sprayed with the cold water, yet they learned to stay away from the ladder and the banana. Why? Because that was the culture; it had always been done that way. Initially the monkeys were reacting to a stimulus from the environment, but the behavior continued even after the stimulus was gone.

That's the way culture gets formed.

CORPORATE CULTURE

Many leaders realize that culture can be an obstacle to making the transition to a new strategy or business model. I had a client firm in the professional services industry that was facing disruptive change in its segment of the industry. The new CEO correctly identified the positive and less than positive aspects of the current culture and the aspects of it that would have to be changed in the new environment. Components of the current culture included high professionalism, integrity, customer focus, and compassion but also inertia, insularity, and a focus on activity and process rather than results. The components necessary to compete in the new dynamic environment included an outward competitive and market focus, accountability, and a bit of risk taking. The CEO was working to stitch the new values into the fabric of the culture, but she was aware it would take time.

Corporate culture gives people a sense of direction, a sense of how to behave in an organization. Even though it's intangible, insiders and outsiders often can describe it, as indicated in the Corporate Culture Matching Quiz that follows. Take a moment to see whether you can match each company with the published description of its culture from the trade press.

Culture can be so firmly embedded in and identified with an organization that the two become almost synonymous, as in the Toyota Way or the

Xerox Way. Thus, the strength of culture can suppress uncertainty. Corporate culture is not right or wrong per se, just right or wrong in the context in which it exists. A strong culture without a guiding vision will perpetuate the status quo. The longer that happens, the more entrenched the culture becomes.

Of course, corporate culture is not universal across an organization. I once worked for a company in which my division was up for sale. I was put in charge of the corporate culture committee to profile the company's culture. (Little did I realize what that meant!) I held informal focus groups and interviewed numerous employees as part of a culture audit. Not surprisingly, there were different subcultures in production, operations, marketing, field sales, and other departments. However, there were some common values that permeated the entire organization and formed the core of the culture. That information became important as the merger process moved forward.

The recognition of these diverse viewpoints of culture throughout the firm spurred me to think differently about the role of leadership (and followership). Perhaps gauging leadership from the perspective of an individual exerting influence over others was too restrictive, and that achievements are often the work of many "unsung heroes." In other words, culture and organizational change are necessarily part of *collective* leadership. A high-performance workplace requires a profound appreciation of "the people side" of business model renewal.

Although difficult, even the most entrenched behaviors can be modified over time. Define what your firm's culture must manifest to fully enable a successful transition to a new strategy or business model. Then consider the emotional factors that must be present during the transition process. Status, trust, certainty, belongingness, transparency, and fairness (or the lack of them) can support (or undermine) your efforts to build a motivated aligned culture.

Think about the cultural attributes that either enhance or inhibit a new business model or strategy from taking root and create a culture map (see Figure 8-1). Note the comparative positions in that figure. The current culture is stable and conservative, with strong team accountability and internal orientation. It is middle of the road in terms of outcome versus process focus and efficient versus conversational with customers. The desired culture would be more innovative, fast-paced, and outcome-focused, with a heightened external orientation and somewhat greater individual accountability.

CORPORATE CULTURE MATCHING QUIZ

All the descriptions of corporate culture were obtained from articles in the business press. Match the culture with the appropriate company on the right. (*Answers can be found at the end of the chapter, preceding the "Reference" section.*)

☐	1.	Investment in research and development is a reflection of corporate culture, and the firm continues to file more patent applications year after year. (*Network World,* Dec. 6, 2010)	Nokia (A)
☐	2.	The company is an acknowledged champion in the cult of fun; "its offices are blessed with volleyball courts, bicycle paths, a yellow brick road, a model dinosaur, regular games of roller hockey and several professional masseuses." (*The Economist,* Sept. 18, 2010)	IBM (B)
☐	3.	The culture was shaped by 10 core values on which it hired and fired. Though it had a playful side, with values such as "create fun and a little weirdness," it pushed performance just as hard with values such as "do more with less," and "deliver 'wow' through services." (*Financial Times,* Feb. 17, 2011)	General Motors (C)
☐	4.	Top management had a history of "greenwashing," or playing up to environmental activists, while taking a cavalier attitude toward risk management. The corporate culture encouraged managers to put profits before safety. (*Weekly Standard,* April 18, 2011; *Pak Banker,* Oct. 20, 2010)	Google (D)
☐	5.	The company has had problems with corporate culture. There has been a lack of urgency and a lack of focus on customers and shareholder value. Insularity combined with arrogance contributed to a toxic culture. (*BusinessWeek,* Aug. 26, 2010)	BP (E)
☐	6.	Company insiders credit the firm's growth to a history of encouraging employees to say whatever's on their minds, with faith that smarter ideas will result. (*BusinessWeek,* June 22, 2009)	Zappos (F)

FIGURE 8-1 ➤ Example of a culture map

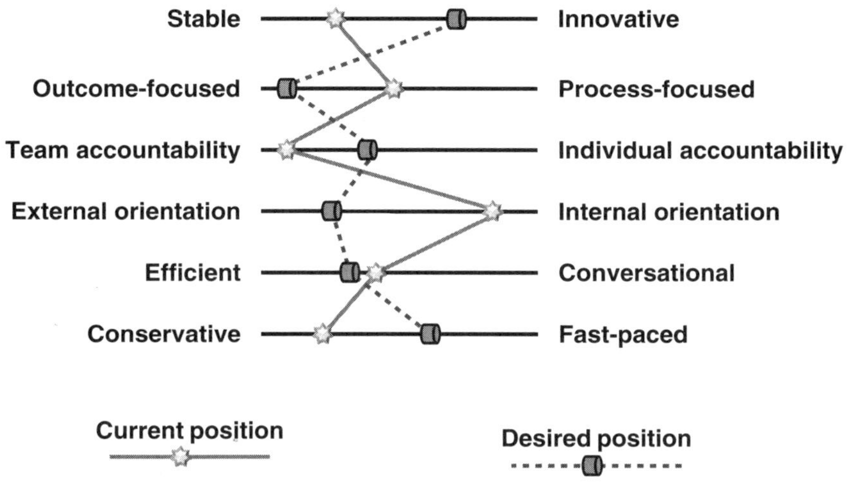

Start by defining relevant characteristics and then ask employees to plot the firm's culture along those characteristics. This can be done by division, department, function, or any other cultural unit involved in the change effort. Next, get agreement from the leadership team on the desired positions for those characteristics. Finally, prioritize which items to focus on and in what order. As Peter Bregman recommended in his blog post, change just one thing at a time.

It's virtually impossible to make a wholesale culture shift in the short term; that kind of shift evolves over time with appropriate guidance, and it requires whole-brain thinking. Think about the competencies and behaviors that need to change but always keep in mind the human side of the equation.

LEADING CHANGE

Change is not an analytical, detached process. It's emotional—sometimes exhilarating and sometimes painful. It's important to remember that change is not necessarily bad, nor is it always resisted. People choose to get married, have children, and enter new careers—all changes that can have profound and long-reaching impacts. The decisions often require significant soul-searching, but they are willingly made. Thus, changes can be positive or at least have more upside than downside consequences. It's up to leaders and change agents to uncover and position the upside of change (or the downside of the status quo).

Who is responsible for leading change depends on the type of change. If it's the transformation of an entire organization, the CEO must lead the charge; a division manager or a department head is responsible if the change involves a more focused group within the company.

John Kotter identified eight critical success factors in leading change: (1) creating a sense of urgency, (2) establishing a strong team to guide the effort, (3) creating a powerful vision, (4) conscientiously disseminating the vision, (5) motivating progress toward the vision, (6) coordinating short-term wins, (7) continuously reinforcing the change, and (8) embedding new components into the culture (see Figure 8-2).

FIGURE 8-2 ➤ Kotter's eight-step change management model

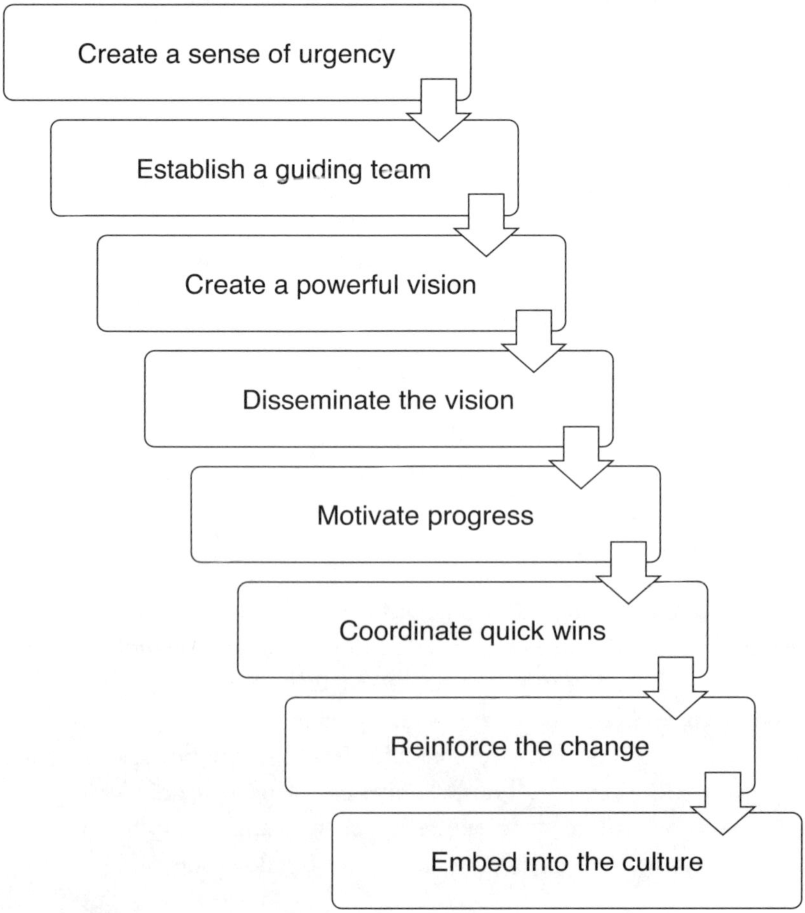

Sense of Urgency

Leaders need to instill a sense of urgency as the foundation for the transformational business case. Without an urgency to act, it's too easy to fall back on the status quo. But sometimes the urgency isn't felt until there is a crisis. This concept is easy to understand, but the ability to spur action can be problematic.

I often show a brief video clip of *Apollo 13* in my executive education classes. In the video, the *Apollo 13* astronauts face a crisis as a result of a CO_2 filter designed for two humans that is unable to filter out the carbon dioxide expelled by the three people. The NASA scientists on the ground work diligently to essentially create a new product, using only materials available on the space module, and complete it before the level of CO_2 harms the astronauts. Obviously, the sense of urgency was high because of the very real life-and-death situation, and so it prompted immediate action.

When the need for action is not as clear-cut, how can you invoke a sense of urgency? It often starts with a frank discussion about the strength of new competition, technological impacts on the rate of obsolescence, or indexes of the firm's declining competitive position. Sometimes the scenario development processes (see Chapter 3) highlights the need for urgency. Strive to demonstrate how the status quo is more dangerous than the alternative of shifting strategy or moving to a new business model. Legitimize the external opportunities to get significant stakeholders on board.

When Nokia hired Stephen Elop, its first non-Finnish CEO, in late 2010, Nokia's smartphone operating system was losing ground to Google and Apple. Elop realized he had to create a sense of urgency to encourage the firm's employees to move away from a failed strategy. He sent a memo to employees in which he told a story about a man who saved his life by jumping off a burning oil platform into the frigid North Sea. He continued, "Nokia, our platform is burning."

For the urgency to be strong enough to motivate action on a major business model transformation, Kotter suggests that it's important that about 75 percent of the firm's management be convinced that business as usual is not acceptable. When a crisis is visible, it's easier to establish a sense of urgency. But that can also mean that action should have been taken sooner.

Guiding Team

It's important to assemble a team with sufficient authority and credibility to lead the effort. For a corporate transformation this may require all of senior leadership; in addition, it may include a board member, a representative from labor, and/or key strategic partners. For a departmental change, it may include a cross section of employees and a higher-level champion.

Organizational alignment has to begin with management alignment. If managers are unaware of the change or uninformed about the expectations going forward, they won't be able to encourage or model the desired behavior or communicate with one voice. This results in conflicting messages and confusion, with people working at cross-purposes.

Depoliticize senior management so that you can loosen control without losing control. In other words, encourage employees and managers to speak with one another without fear of political repercussions. Expose your senior managers to frontline perspectives to be sure the point of view of frontline employees is heard.

Powerful Vision

As we've already seen, a vision is more than numbers. It's an important mental image of what the future could be, and it also should define the preferred future culture necessary to achieve the desired results. The vision becomes the central hub for the various initiatives that enable it. Without this central vision, strategies dissolve into a mix of confusing and incompatible projects.

To be powerful, a vision statement has to be contextually relevant. Komatsu's vision statement (essentially "Beat Caterpillar"), as was discussed in Chapter 7, resonated with the employees when the firm was a small equipment manufacturer in Japan, and it provided future direction for almost two decades. But as Komatsu grew to be a global player, the vision became restrictive (since it focused almost exclusively on benchmarking against Caterpillar) and no longer served its function of encouraging strategic thinking.

The American Physical Therapy Association (APTA) has a vision statement (as well as the strategic plan to achieve that vision) on its website. Although the APTA is a membership organization rather than a corporation, it has to generate revenue through membership fees, operate in a complex regulatory and competitive environment, and deal with both allies and resisters to its strategies. As a result, there may be some ideas to be gleaned in the development of its vision and strategies. The short version of the vision statement, endorsed in 2000, is as follows:

> *By 2020, physical therapy will be provided by physical therapists who are doctors of physical therapy, recognized by consumers and other health care professionals as the practitioners of choice to whom consumers have direct access for the diagnosis of, interventions for, and prevention of impairments, activity limitations, participation restrictions, and environmental barriers related to movement, function, and health.*

A vision statement highlights the end point of a journey for the organization; strategies provide the road map to get there. Most statements contain (or imply) the words *to become*, referring to some future point in time. They probably specify where you want the organization to be positioned (e.g., a leader in design, innovation, technology, etc.), what "sandboxes" you want to play in (e.g., countries, industries, or markets), and the type of corporate culture that will exist. They should be inspirational to stakeholders, balanced between being overly narrow (restricting the ability to take advantage of opportunities) and overly broad (providing absolutely no differentiation in direction), and easily understandable after no more than five minutes of discussion.

It is usually easiest (and most successful) for the statement to be written by one individual, with input from multiple stakeholders before, during, and after the writing.

Share the Vision

Getting people excited enough to buy into a vision requires more than a couple of PowerPoint presentations and a story in the company newsletter. Even if they are dissatisfied with the status quo, people aren't likely to make short-term sacrifices unless they truly believe useful change is possible.

Interface, a global manufacturer of modular carpet, has a stated vision on its website: "To be the first company that, by its deeds, shows the entire industrial world what sustainability is in all its dimensions: people, process, product, place and profits—by 2020—and in doing so we will become restorative through the power of influence." The story behind this vision is interesting.

Ray Anderson, the founder and CEO, introduced the concept of sustainability at the company's annual meeting in 1994. He admits that at the time the company was expecting him to discuss compliance, legal requirements, and the financial situation, and his message was a surprise. But that speech was a first step in communicating and **sharing his vision.** He challenged the

http://www.interfaceglobal.com/getdoc/7004276e–0f10–4c64-b08c-b7889a717b2b/Ray-Reflects.aspx

company to move toward, in his words, "that mystical place called sustainability." He presented his vision at every opportunity: plant meetings, sales meetings, and individual discussions. His goal was to change one mind at a time in this company with 3,000 people and encourage employees to internalize the vision. He also provided a business case showing that costs were down rather than up as a result of the vision and stated that the wellspring of sustainable design had resulted in innovative products for their customers.

True transformation is not possible unless hundreds or thousands of employees are onboard and willing to help. Without credible and multiple communications, the hearts and minds of the stakeholders will not be persuaded. Sharing the vision implies two-directional communication. Not only do leaders talk about their visions, they must listen to the inputs and concerns of the various stakeholders.

Different executives have imparted to me their approaches to communicating their vision across the organization or department. Many subtly build the message into their daily conversations with employees. Some send a quarterly e-mail report "from the future." The e-mail describes what the company is "doing" on that future date and serves as a reminder of the vision. Others are more apt to use a cascading approach in which each manager from the top to the front line verbally shares the vision with his or her direct reports. Many incorporate educational events in which elements of the vision are infused into the instruction. Virtually all of them attested to the importance of role modeling any changes that might be required for the vision to take root.

Don't worry about redundancy. People need to hear the message several times before it is truly heard. And it's usually a good idea for the message to be communicated through more than one medium. The bottom line is that the best approach to use is the one that works within your culture.

Motivate Progress

After the vision and high-level strategies have been shared, you'll find that some people actively embrace the change. Some people initially reject it but eventually come around. Some go through the motions but continue with the status quo. Unfortunately, some actively resist and campaign against any changes. No matter how clear you thought the vision was and how supportive the employees were, there will be surprises. And there will always be traditionalists who find any shift virtually blasphemous.

Cultural alignments must be both leadership-driven and grassroots-enabled. The more people involved, the better the outcome. As I mentioned earlier, most organizations have subcultures in different departments and units. Getting support from diverse constituents increases the likelihood that there will be progress toward the new vision. Build your A team of people most likely to be catalysts and champions of the new direction and encourage them to stimulate progress.

FIGURE 8-3 ➤ Frustration sets it

Think about why and how people might resist change efforts and work to reduce the negatives. At some point it's likely that frustration will set in for everyone (see Figure 8-3). Be prepared to occasionally take a step back to regroup and refocus on the future.

Leaders should try to identify any constraints that may be impeding progress and work to remove the obstacles. Do job descriptions need to be rewritten? If new skills have to be developed or additional competencies are required, it may help to develop a competency scorecard to determine the types of changes necessary. Figure 8-4 shows a product manager competency model as an example.

Look for ways to build desired competencies as painlessly and successfully as possible. P&G and Google, for example, swapped two dozen employees for a few weeks. P&G wanted its employees to learn more about online capabilities, and Google wanted to gain insights into brand building.

Assess whether the current structures (and reporting relationships) are appropriate for the new future. Commit resources (such as time, money, training, and expertise) for pilot projects and subsequent change initiatives. Although it's impossible to eliminate all barriers, at least the most prominent need to be dealt with.

Remember that employees have questions in their minds, whether or not they voice them. Following are common questions. Think about how you would answer these questions. As Interface's Ray Anderson suggested, successful change occurs one mind at a time. Although it's unlikely that these questions

FIGURE 8-4 ➤ Example of a product manager competency model

Drive business results		Deliver results through people		Create strategies		Ensure market-driven direction		Guide product "fit" and function		Manage multiple priorities		Exhibit enterpreneurial traits	
Financial aptitude		Leadership		Ability to spot trends		Market analysis & segmentation		Technical know-how		Project management skills		Self-discipline	
Selling knowledge & skills		Influence & motivation		Product portfolio building		Competitive intelligence		New product development knowledge		Time management skills		Visionary	
Business planning		Team management		Long-term foresight		Go-to-market knowledge		Quality assurance		Organized		Risk tolerance	
Forecasting		Decision-making		Ability to deal with ambiguity		Customer champion		Product line fit		Ability to execute plans		Can-do attitude	
Process know-how		Perceptive		Partnerships		Brand and message fit		Prototype validation		Ability to say no when necessary		Results-oriented	
Total Weighted Scores													

Weight of the specific competency

Rating of product manager on the specified competency

Scores based on the sum of the weight x rating numbers

Skill level ratings:

1. *Deficient.* Product manager lacks some of the necessary experience, skills, or abilities related to this competence.
2. *Basically Competent.* Product manager is able to perform these competencies on a fundamental level and understand the knowledge to be able to participate in decision-making.
3. *Proficient.* Product manager is able to perform these competencies on a fully operational level and understand them well enough to teach others, if necessary.
4. *Advanced.* Product manager is not only proficient in these competencies, but also pushes the competency to a higher level.

can truly be answered on an individual basis, think in terms of departments or other units closer to the individuals.

- How is this change relevant to what I do?
- What specifically should I do?
- How will I be measured, and what consequences will I face?
- What tools and support are available?
- What's in it for me?

Coordinate Short-Term Wins

Since business model renewal is a long-term process, there is a time lag between when the vision is first articulated and when change becomes visible. Consequently, people begin to fall back into their old habits if they don't see any identifiable results. To be "real," the results have to be unambiguous.

Look for opportunities to showcase success such as increased customer satisfaction, growth in targeted markets, or innovative products that match the change initiative. But also consider ways to engineer success whenever possible. The first approach is passive, and the second is active.

Continuously Reinforce the Direction

Short-term wins deserve celebration, but they should not be mistaken for reaching the goalpost. Ironically, too much celebration can kill the momentum. Remind people that though progress has been made, the vision has not yet been achieved.

A caution about continuously reinforcing the direction: It can cause endless meetings at which people struggle to find consensus.

Embed the Required Culture

Culture evolves in a subtle (almost stealth) manner. Change sticks when it becomes "the way we do things around here." Encourage employees to collaborate with people they don't normally interact with. Not only does this help morph the culture, it can be a springboard for grassroots innovation.

Change initiatives that are scheduled to be completed in a relatively short time have the greatest likelihood of success. If completing the change is going to take a significant amount of time, it's important to build milestones and regular reviews into the structure of the change program.

KALEIDOSCOPE OR BINOCULARS

Many bureaucracies approach change management with the same rigidity applied to all operations. Business analysis is conducted to determine the gap between the existing position and the desired position. A change management program is enacted with written procedures and standards detailed. Requirements and specifications are documented. Resources are committed, and the program is deployed.

Although this approach makes sense, there are two potential shortcomings. First, the time it takes to implement a cumbersome change management plan can be considerable. Second, the plan usually presumes one particular end point whereas in rapidly changing environments there may be several probable futures. How should a company proceed? If we categorize the change into incremental versus radical and the future options as limited (perhaps one) versus multiple possibilities, we can create a diagram of change options (see Figure 8-5).

When the direction of a shift is focused, it's possible to use well-researched approaches to change management. John Kotter's eight-step process is a very common methodology for larger transitions. Smaller redirections (say, within a department) probably will follow a more streamlined approach, even though it most likely will be thematically similar.

The future is not always clear, so the challenge of organizational change becomes greater. That is when companies need a test-and-learn culture. For smaller incremental changes, say, product innovations that don't require a business model

FIGURE 8-5 ➤ Change kaleidoscope

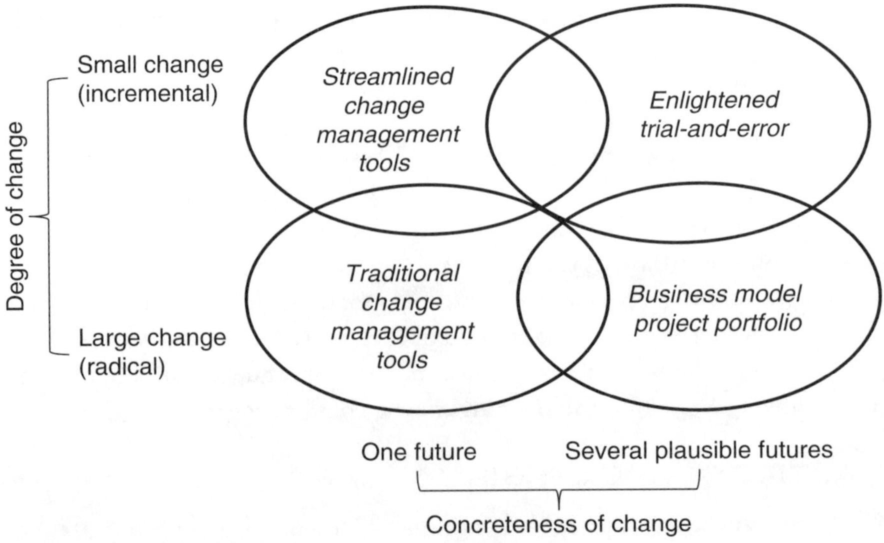

change, enlightened trial and error is appropriate. Ongoing testing and refinement of alpha and beta prototypes allows firms to hedge their bets when customer and market trends are dynamic and unpredictable.

The final circle refers to innovations requiring business model transformations when the future is unknowable. Sometimes this means building breakthrough businesses within established organizations, potentially causing a clash of NewCo and CoreCo cultures. We saw in Chapter 4 the challenge Xerox faced in creating a computer ecosystem business at its PARC facility (NewCo) when the organizational structures, systems, and mindsets were based on the corporate copying business (CoreCo).

In theory a NewCo should have some advantages over an independent start-up by virtue of access to assets such as facilities and money from the CoreCo, but several challenges can outweigh the advantages. There may be different customer targets, mental models, technologies, incentives, job descriptions, and/or cultures between these business units. That means they are not likely to coexist gracefully. How can management calm the waters?

First, redefine success metrics so that they are relevant and appropriate for each business model. Don't play games to benefit one over the other but realistically determine expectations on the basis of the environmental context as well as the strategic value of each business unit to the firm. Then build a dashboard for NewCo. Second, don't assign status on the basis of the current size of the business model. That will almost always put NewCo at a disadvantage. Third, think in terms of a portfolio. Recognize that its value may be some combination of sustaining, transformative, and disruptive growth models.

CORPORATE CULTURE AND BUSINESS MODEL RENEWAL

The final question is, How do you change culture to fit with business model renewal? That's actually several questions. Begin by determining whether wholesale change is necessary. As was mentioned before, there are usually subcultures in any organization, and if you have a business model portfolio mindset, it may be possible to fit different business models with different cultures. There also may be the possibility of building on strong components of an existing culture that fit with the new business models.

But how should a firm approach more widespread cultural change? There are two significant schools of thought on that. One believes that changing thoughts will lead to new behaviors, and the other believes that changing behavior will lead to a new mindset. In reality, it's probably some of both. I often ask executives whether they have ever been on a diet or another self-improvement regimen. Most have. When I dig deeper into which ones resulted in sustained change, they were generally the ones that were incorporated into day-to-day life rather than being bolted on. The same is true for cultural change. There is usually an awareness component (vision and sense of urgency), along with ongoing incentives to promote new behaviors (rather than temporary programs and measures.)

To have the adaptability to pursue the test-and-learn approach to business model portfolios, cultures themselves have to be remodeled to embrace this philosophy. They must foster change as business as usual. The organizational structure, processes, and reward systems must support implementation and reimplementation of strategies on a continual basis. Job descriptions must focus on the individual's responsibility to learn and adapt rather than simply repeat a task over and over. Reward systems must encourage individual development and reskilling. The structure must put as many people in contact with the external environment as possible, and leadership should be dispersed throughout the organization. With these factors in place, companies can shift from simply asking themselves what they do well to asking themselves what they need to learn and what competencies they need to develop to be prepared for continual business model renewal.

JOAN FINLEY

ORCHESTRATING BUSINESS MODEL RENEWAL THROUGH EFFECTIVE ORGANIZATIONAL CHANGE INITIATIVES

Dr. Joan Finley's focus is on assisting teams in tapping into their passion and strengths to drive change and progressive results. Joan facilitates strategic change management by using leading models such as the Influencer Model, Values in Action (VIA), and StrengthsFinder 2.0, all of which are mindful and deliberate positive techniques that result in sustainable change for organizations. She collaborates with leaders to drive sustainable change by blending organization change practices with project management disciplines. Joan can be contacted at finley.joan@yahoo.com and 847–212–8062.

Joan Finley, Ph.D.
Senior Program Manager
Baxter Healthcare

Joan, can you start us out with the basics by explaining how organizational development as a discipline or philosophy differs from other systems of organizational change?

In general, organizational development (also known as OD) is an organization-wide effort to guide both systematic and systemic progress toward some goal. Of course, it means different things to different people. Some people consider the work of OD professionals to be distinctly different from that of human resources (HR) professionals, with a responsibility for activities such as team building, structural alignment, and change management. Other people believe OD has already been absorbed into HR. Still others think OD is not about change at all but more about preserving the status quo.

But if we look at it from a change perspective, it can involve *reactively* helping employees respond to necessary strategy or business model shifts or *proactively* preparing employees to adapt to future transitions. From a reactive perspective, OD is probably quite similar to other approaches to change management in which the focus is on leaders driving their visions through the firm and convincing employees to buy into it. The proactive side of OD differentiates it a bit from other systems of organizational change because the efforts are focused more on ongoing interventions to increase a firm's readiness to change. Organizational development provides the vehicle for organizations to migrate from one paradigm to another by grooming change agents to help them play a role in moving an organization forward.

You mentioned the importance of a change agent. Can you elaborate on that a bit?

Sure. Change agents are critical to engaging the people who are involved in the changes that leaders and stakeholders are driving forward. They are the opinion leaders who proactively engage those people, facilitating the new paradigms and the human bridge from the past to the future. As bridge builders, change agents must determine what needs to be in place for successful and sustainable change to occur. They become the support system—the safety net—for those in the organization as they go from denial, to exploration, to acceptance, to inspiration and being drivers of change. They are the underpinnings of any successful change as they inspire collaboration and camaraderie through social connectedness.

Change can exist along a continuum from relatively small-scale projects to almost existence-altering complexity. Business model changes almost always lean toward the complex side. How can the knowledge of OD help companies manage that level of complexity?

The knowledge of organization development assists companies in navigating through the complex social network connections and required tailored communications and change strategies to drive the desired results. Many times there are behaviors which are not aligned with desired results. Organization scientists have identified various assessments to diagnose the types of strategies which will work in various situations. Knowledge and experience with the latest working theories and assessments can lead to efficient and effective change management.

Earlier you mentioned collaboration. How have you enhanced collaboration within organizations?

I have enhanced collaboration through orchestrating the right conversations at the right time. Through identification of the interdependencies to drive the change requirements, I have caught the attention of the leaders, making them aware of various changes required to get results. I've developed change strategies that are based on evolving behaviors so that they are aligned with the designed results.

I've engaged the training folks to include from and to situations, providing initial context to those we expected to change. I've discussed the requirements I have of the leaders as well as the rest of the team to achieve the change. I've orchestrated presentations so that the leaders or the team members will present provocative information on ideas for change, leading to important conversations.

That leads us to culture. Can the change and collaboration efforts you described work in any culture?

The change strategies I mentioned above can be used in any culture, but only with knowledge of how the culture will process them. That means they must be tailored to the cultural leadership style. One must be very careful, mindful of leadership styles, so that the change management efforts are not shut down. Engaging people in the various cultures and discussing their perceptions is something I found imperative.

In your opinion, are company executives more likely to fail when they implement a "wrong" strategy that's consistent with their culture or when they implement a "right" strategy that's inconsistent with their culture?

It depends. If they implement the strategy which is wrong but right for the culture, it will be successful in the short term and not in the long term. The executives require organization development assistance to implement the right strategy which is inconsistent with the culture.

Are there any final words of advice you can provide to managers and executives who are attempting a business model transformation that requires significant organizational change?

For change to occur effectively and in a timely manner, it is imperative to acknowledge both the leaders and the workforce. Application of positive change management techniques can drive innovation and change in a sustainable manner. I also advise that executives be patient with the workforce and model the change they wish to see.

ANSWERS TO THE CORPORATE CULTURE MATCHING QUIZ

Answers: 1-B, 2-D, 3-F, 4-E, 5-C, 6-A

REFERENCES

Bregman, Peter, "To Change Effectively, Change Just One Thing," blog post, peterbregman.com, October 6, 2009.

Coy, Peter, "Shareholder Alert: The State of the Business Is Not Good," *Bloomberg Businessweek*, February 28–March 6, 2011, pp. 51–56.

Kotter, John P., "Leading Change: Why Transformation Efforts Fail," *Harvard Business Review*, January 2007, pp. 96–103.

Shook, John, "How to Change a Culture: Lessons from NUMMI," *MIT Sloan Management Review*, Winter 2010, pp. 63–68.

Taylor, William C., *Practically Radical: Not-So-Crazy Ways to Transform Your Company, Shake Up Your Industry, and Challenge Yourself*, William Morrow, 2011.

Worley, Christopher G., and Edward E. Lawler III, "Designing Organizations That Are Built to Change," *MIT Sloan Management Review*, Fall 2006, pp. 19–23.

Index

About the Author

Linda Gorchels is a member of the Executive Education faculty in the University of Wisconsin–Madison's School of Business, where she has conducted training for over 10,000 corporate executives across the United States and globally. She is the award-winning author of *The Product Manager's Handbook* and *The Product Manager's Field Guide*, and has worked with organizations such as Trane Commercial Systems, GE Medical, Siemens, Metso Automation, Nokia (in Beijing), J.F. Pearson (in Shanghai), Elkay and Kerry Ingredients, among others.